SKYCAR CITY

A Pre-emptive History

MVRDV | UWM

Edited by
Winy Maas and Grace La

With
Ryan O'Connor, Trevor Patt, Nick Popoutsis, Andy Walsh

Students
Bryan Howard, Tony Janis, Nick Moen, Ryan O'Connor, Ella Peinovich, Trevor Patt, Nick Popoutsis, Tarah Raaum, Gloribed Rivera-Torres, Scott Schultz, Tuan Tran, and Andy Walsh.

The skycar first appeared in the pages of *Popular Mechanics* over a century ago in April 1906, nearly fifteen years after it was first imagined in the illustrations of Albert Robida. Following the Wright brothers' flyer by only three years, and Karl Benz's automobile by seven years, respectively, the concept of the

skycar has persisted for over a century in film, literature, illustration, world fairs, and comic books: it is an icon of "the future."

The architectural discourse contains a rich history of future projections presented via city designs. This tradition has its root in early Modernism, during a time

when the city was synonymous with Modernist promises and shortcomings. The architects of this era proposed visionary cities that broke with more dire city visions of crowded streets and the "intensification of nervous stimuli,"[1] in favor of transportation infrastructure.

More receptive to the machine aesthetic's veneration of efficiency, infrastructure (or the flow of transportation) was both a metaphor for the flux of society and an 'object' that was simultaneously coming and going, formless and siteless, a model of the Einsteinian world where transportation infrastructure channelled and optimized.

The quantifiable nature of traffic enabled infrastructure to so powerfully dominate actual elements of the city, that St. Elia's Città Nuova exists only at those nodes where transportation and information infrastructures intersect. The sum of such designs came to a close with Frank Lloyd Wright's Broadacre City: a model marked by the

ubiquity of suburbanism, the ironic result of the city's subordination by infrastructure. An interesting movement, at the urban scale, reappears in the visionary architecture of the 1960's. Here infrastructure is not employed in the service of efficiency and rationality, but rather in the pursuit of freedom and transformation

Rather than the heroic forms of Modernism, these cities propose environments
responsive to actual situations and their citizens.
An integrated transportation infrastructure, such as the crane/rail system
in Plug-in City, predisposes the city toward its own addition, removal, and

transformation, empowering its citizens to push the city "into the shape people want it to be rather than [the inverse]."[2] Proposals such as Walking City and even Superstudio's Continuous Conveyer Belt City, put forth a city that retains a consistent identity but dissociates itself from its geographic location, offering

a freedom of place and site. These projects seem to avoid the tension inherent in Modernism's struggle between creation and destruction by invoking a planned obsolescence. They are not based in the object world of the machine-aesthetic, but in the fluid realm of media and advertising. Interestingly, the infrastructures

of these cities, though they facilitate transformations of the city, do not themselves transform, but rather provide a sort of "deep structure" around which urban form changes and evolves.

Recently, advances in computer animation software have allowed a number of visionary cities to be realized in film. These cities are similar to the illustrations of the "city of the future" (as imagined just after the turn of the last century); these cities are spirited, imaginative, yet are still simply images.

Growing interest in systems and processes has reintroduced infrastructure
into contemporary architecture discoure. Now, research-based practices are
utilizing infrastructure and design to address issues currently facing cities:
overpopulation, density, resources, pollution, congestion, increasing privatization.

Skycar City is positioned at the confluence of these issues, speculating on urban transportation infrastructure as a medium through which to imagine the potentials of the new city, one where movement is both efficient and free.

1   The Metropolis and Mental Life. Georg Simmel. tr. Kurt Wolff in *The Sociology of Georg Simmel*. p. 409

2   www.partner-blue.de/text_lectures/0510_UniRiga/051104_mega_handout.pdf. Markus Schlosser,
    quoted from *The London Sunday Times*, 1964. No date or authorship cited.

CONTENTS

FOREWORD
Robert Greenstreet

In May of 2005, a five-person jury convened at the University of Wisconsin-Milwaukee School of Architecture & Urban Planning to select the first recipient of the Marcus Prize, a new, bi-annual architectural award funded by the Marcus Corporation Foundation. The award recognizes emerging talent in the world of architecture. A distinguished pool of international nominators identified 22 candidates, representing nine different countries and a broad spectrum of design agendas. From this pool and following extensive deliberations, the jury selected the Rotterdam firm of MVRDV.

In addition to the award itself, the Marcus Corporation Foundation provided financial support to host the competition and to bring the awardees to Milwaukee to run an academic design studio in collaboration with UWM faculty. This book is the result of the first Marcus Prize Studio, led by Winy Maas (principal of MVRDV), and Grace La (Associate Professor at UWM). This teaching dyad was a conscious pairing of two energetic individuals, a productive match of vitality and commitment to the pedagogical research of architecture within the academy. Their ability to inspire, to experiment, and to work fluently between architectural research and design, initiated our desire to document the studio's efforts. This publication, the first in an intended series of Marcus Prize Studio publications, disseminates the results of the Marcus Prize program overall and hopes to contribute to dialogue in research, experimentation, and practice of architecture.

The Marcus Prize studio, comprised of twelve graduate and undergraduate students, undertook the semester-long investigation in the spring of 2006, exploring the relationship between infrastructure, architecture, and urban form. The studio's process was highly collaborative in nature, multi-disciplinary in approach, and theoretical in essence. The UWM students' work represents a milestone in studio cooperation, utilizing every available technology to support pedagogical intent and placing this design research squarely within the body of global discourse. We are grateful to the Marcus Corporation Foundation for their support and inception of this award and to Winy Maas, Grace La, the Marcus Prize Studio, and the student editors, Ryan O'Connor, Trevor Patt, Nick Popoutsis, and Andy Walsh, for their commitment to the making of this work.

Robert Greenstreet, Dean
University of Wisconsin-Milwaukee,
School of Architecture & Urban Planning

SKYCAR CITY
WINY MAAS

"**SKYCAR CITY** is to be expected soon. It will study the dramatic possibilities of the usage of sky-cars, freely moving in between buildings. This will lead to a city with "streets" on any level, or perhaps it is a city even completely without streets."
(KM3, MVRDV, p.472)

FUTURISM Don't we all dream of the future and its sediments, the future cities? What kind of cities will they be? How will they look? On what basis do we form our fantasies? How will cities adapt to major changes? Will global warming create sheltered and protected cities? And what will happen when the cities are occupied by evolved types of human species that require other habitats? And what if there is "outer life" that enters our domains? Or what if there are new technologies?

INSIDE OR OUT? These types of speculations are often positioned "outside" architecture, in the world of filmmakers, dreamers, and parvenus. But is this separation useful? We frequently notice that futuristic visions indirectly occur in architectural realizations. Can a better liaison perhaps be created between the two again? Does this liaison form a sincere "projective architecture?"

TECHNOLOGICAL CHANGES Let us follow the technological trajectory of this concept. Perhaps it follows a classic belief in technology and becomes a technocracy.
What happens to our cities in the face of radical technological change? How can we imagine these technological changes, changes that still do not exist? In the nineteenth century, could people have imagined that cars would dominate the urban landscape? Who could predict the enormous influence of digital technology on urban organizations? When did we imagine that flight and air travel would transform global coexistence?
Maybe there are some scenarios for technological innovation. In moments of scarcity, innovations are required to solve the demands. By addressing these "demands," new technologies emerge. Societal models can influence the approaches of technological changes that range from ignoring, protecting, pushing to facilitating; that lead to a series of technological innovations.

INFRASTRUCTURE One of the dominant drivers behind urban processes is infrastructure. Investments in infrastructure for individual cars, pedestrians, and for public transport lead to greater requirements for accessibility and thus to unimagined economic potentials.

The definition of a city has clearly followed the technological potential: In the Middle Ages, cities measured more or less 5 kilometers in diameter (one hour of walking); in the 1950's, 15 kilometers (one hour of cycling), in the 1980's 100 kilometers (one hour of driving), in the 2000's, 500 kilometers (one hour of flying). What will happen to urbanism when infrastructural means radically change?

SKYCARS From the despair of commuters during rush hours or in times of emergencies, let us construct a hypothesis: that cars 'fly.' How will this hypothesis affect our cities? Could skycars solve current weaknesses and negative connotations: skycars that are environmentally friendly, noiseless, affordable.? What if skycars could move freely between buildings, over landscapes, for everybody. Everywhere...

URBAN CHANGE The space that is currently required for infrastructure "evaporates" substantially! For example, over half the area of Manhattan Island is covered by roads. As a result, only 44% of the ground plane is available for development. Skycars would make streets redundant! They would cease to exist!

This shift quite possibly leads to a city with "streets" on every level. Or maybe even completely without streets. It creates a city without (initially) traffic control! In this city, traffic lights are replaced with a car's onboard navigational system. Parking problems disappear as cars park directly in the sky, hooked or docked to all types of programmatic elements, in any location. Orientation radically changes: the city no longer uses axes or streets, but develops a completely

revolutionized address system based on coordinates. A city without signals, all navigation regulated via the skycar screen…
Destinations feel closer. Time becomes more intense.
The city becomes bigger, denser. Skycar City.

SKYCAR REQUIREMENTS To have this skycar city requires specific demands for the new cars and as well, these new cars will dictate the potentials of the new city's form. Following mutations of existing cars, skycars need other engines that allow for higher speed as well as for "standstills." The skycar will have high aerodynamic performance as well as hover devices that perhaps include operable wings. The skycar has smaller wheels as it does not come in contact with the ground nearly as much. The car also has a panoramic cockpit, to increase visibility and safety in a new driving environment where other skycars can emerge from anywhere, not only from the front, the side, or the back, but also from below as above. A panoramic cockpit is coupled with a seating area that can swivel in all directions. A navigation system that is designed to be even more centrally located. The skycar is completed with a safety system of three-dimensional bumpers, which allow for speed and evasive maneuvering when other objects become (too) close. The shock absorption qualities of these bumpers fluctuate according to real-time traffic densities. With new energy sources and other type of fueling equipment and systems, the skycar is very different from its terrestrial predecessor.

HISTORY A sequence of technological developments form the trajectory of the skycar: the fuel engine, the aircraft, the helicopter, and now new types of energy (hydrogen), noise protection (quiet whispering motors), compacter engines, safety and control equipment, and navigation tools.
Can we expect the "final" skycar developments to occur before 2030?

3D URBANISM Such an invention requires a sincere "new urbanism." Currently, cities are constructed in a more or less two-dimensional way. Zoning determines urban planning and protects cities from true densification. This issue becomes increasingly urgent in times of future spatial scarcity with the development of massive space desires and spatial clustering. The skycar liberates current two-dimensional zoning and enlarges the potential for truly three-dimensional cities and thus for greater capacities.

SKYCAR CATALOG A catalog of skycars has been developed based on different sets of desires.
Options range from the car's speed, to varied configurations including family cars with sedans that absorb all possible even contradictory demands and from skyVespas to skybuses...

SKYCAR CITY 'NEUFERT' How will this skycar city appear? What shape will it take?
Its varied movements and speeds create other maximizations of space. Initially, under current spatial circumstances, a city of free movement can be considered. Here movement is determined by program positioning.
However, as densification continues, more and more air-control requirements are implemented. In the initial years of skycar city, automatic systems can meet this demand, but as the city grows and develops, three-dimensional zoning appears: main tracks and side zones, fast tracks, slow zones.
What paths are to be imagined? How should we begin to design their dimensions? What length, what sectional measurements? Cars can be not only in front or behind but as well to the left and to the right and below and above!
How should we begin to imagine the requisite safety zone that surrounds the skycar, a zone that would ensure easy maneuverability? What if there is a sudden need to move

manually (in case of emergency), requiring visual, individual control? What would be the optimal buffer zone dimension? A cone of "emptiness" surrounds the vehicle (asymmetric in nature due to the difference in reaction times). What is the character of these "empty bubbles?" What is their overlap? What happens when a car must shift from one track to the other? What nodes or intersections can be imagined?

DETAILS In the details we find new and remarkable reconsiderations. What is parking? Is it a docking station? A rack? Does it float? And a house? Will that not change drastically? One can park anywhere, as easily next to the bedroom as adjacent to the kitchen…

PUBLIC SPACE And the public space? How will that be formed? What gatherings can be imagined? As swarms of cars surround performances and spectacles at the opera, the cinema, the aquarium, or the stadium…
And do we want cars to be everywhere? Should we introduce car-free zones? Where are they situated? Can they then be regarded as new national parks?

5 MILLION CITY A contemporary region of five million inhabitants is the reference for the modeling of a dense skycar city.
The calculated program of this city is based on those first suggested in KM3. This city has a reasonable height (800 meters, based on current technologies) and a reasonable density (similar to that of today's Manhattan) to allow for sufficient light.
The program is distributed within this zone, so that everyone can reach the desired destination equally and as fast as possible.
The origins (i.e. homes) are also everywhere.
All other destinations are clustered according to current critical economical sizes. The usages of the destinations are based on current time patterns.

This input creates a predetermined distribution of the needed program with a very visible network of connections, where the density expectations of movements can be calculated.

This leads to trajectories or "streets" with clearly quantifiable usages: a density of individual movements. Imagine that we all have a private skycar –then the potential required "skyspace" can be calculated per street and per section of that street.

Nodes that surround the most frequented areas can be dimensioned appropriately.

All remaining space can be used for housing…

We engaged in an iterative process to create the densest city imaginable.

If the remaining space is filled with program, then ten times the population can be housed but would live in darkness.

This leads to a substantial enlargement and redistribution of the various traffic zones…

Housing is placed parallel to the skypaths in concentric bands to create a kind of "onion ring" model city, which allows for thin houses to connect with more quiet "streets."

If all housing is placed adjacent to the skypaths, they can be used to create car-free zones in between: a garden city emerges. As polyps are planned around these skytracks, cul-de-sac spaces are created for low speed areas and within surrounding communities. Voids between the parks are created to create access and links between the parks. This smaller scale circulation could be reserved for skyVespas and skybikes.

FOLLOW UP: SMALL JET CITY Currently one can observe the eminent development of small jets. More and more people use them. They can land on short landing strips and can cross distances up to 1500 kilometers. What will be the next step in this development?

Imagine that one can reach a plane everywhere within one hour for a reasonable price in any direction. How many airstrips do we need? Where do we position this airstrip? What additional infrastructure is required to achieve this goal? In especially dense metropolitan zones this challenge becomes an intriguing puzzle. It suggests the development of a "grid" of small airports, located at intervals of every 40 kilometers.

What consequences do they have on the airspace? How do they mingle with the existing one? Do they reduce the size of the intercontinental hubs?

What consequences do they have for the city? How about noise? Should there be strict skypaths?

(to be continued…)

URBAN CHANGE
DENSITY
SITUATIONS

Liberated from the confines of the groundplane, the advantages and potentials of a sky-based circulation infrastructure transforms the notion of commuting and moving throughout the city. This paradigm shift also utterly revamps the way in which our cities evolve and grow.

On the ground, cars dominate!

Ratio of road and parking area to built area on the ground plane of Manhattan:

56:1

Manhattan, NY USA. 2006

In the city and suburbs, roads envelop all surfaces, a seemingly endless network.

Current development models maximize property road access either through a street grid or, as in much of suburban America, by snaking roads through subdivisions. Though this maximizes edge length, the surface area of the roads has

increased exponen- tially,

creating inefficient property to road ratios.

Milwaukee, WI USA. 2006

What if all the pavement vanished?

Transportation infrastructure

Overwhelms

The Creative Potential within Cities!

Miller Park, Milwaukee, WI USA

And the entire network disappeared?

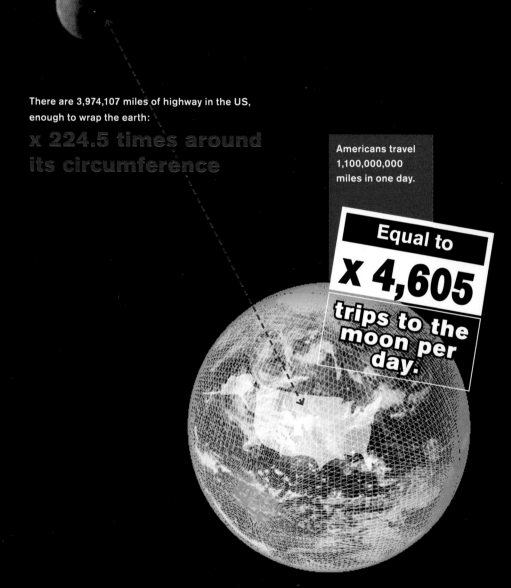

There are 3,974,107 miles of highway in the US, enough to wrap the earth:

x 224.5 times around its circumference

Americans travel 1,100,000,000 miles in one day.

Equal to
x 4,605
trips to the moon per day.

What are the limitations and costs of our transportation infrastructure?

Despite the enormous area dedicated to cars within the city and the landscape, roads still suffer from congestion. In dense cities inhabitants return to a single level in order to move laterally. In the suburbs, the intense hierarchy of the road networks and the disconnection of neighborhoods places stress on the primary roads, while feeder streets remain underutilized. In 2003, congestion delayed U.S. travelers 79 million more hours and wasted 69 million more gallons of fuel than in 2002.

This congestion is worth $3,910,0000 in total wasted gasoline at the 2002 price of $1.70 per gallon. Assuming no increase in congestion, this yields $6.97 billion of wasted gasoline at 2007 prices of $3.03 per gallon.

New York City, NY USA. 2006

Is there an alternative to the current and

The United States' annual expenditure for national highway improvements and maintenance is:

$30,024,236,000

New Orleans, LA USA. 2006

costly situation that now dominates?

The national indebtedness in the United States due to automobile infrastructure is:

$119,570,826,000

Dallas, TX USA. 2004

Where is the untapped potential?

Over half of Manhattan Island is covered by roads. As a result only 44% of the ground plane is available for development. Considering the total volume of unbuilt space above the ground reveals a different story. Compared to the built volume, open space makes up over four times as much volume.
At a potential $430 per square foot of air space, the real estate value for this volume would be approximately:

$10,700,000,000

This provides an economic incentive for a more three-dimensional city, but problems of access to these properties remain.

air Volume - based on current
value of Manhattan property
$430 US Dollars / ft2
24,560,377,237 ft³

Manhattan, NY USA. 2006

Ratio of
air volume
to built
volume
4.1:1

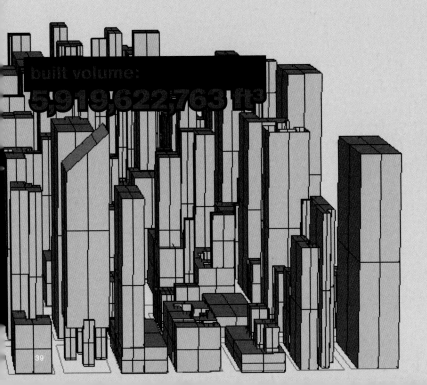

built volume:
5,919,622,763 ft³

Why not take advantage of all the real estate above?

This is the story of Skycar City.

FROM CAR
TO SKYCAR

The advent of new and existing technologies, fueled by human fascination with flight, offers a foundation from which to imagine skycar. While the concept of skycar appears elusive, the technology is emerging in several different aeronautical projects.

SKYCAR FAMILY TREE / Man's Quest for Personal Flight

Desire for mobility is a the thread through transportation lineage. Ground transportation, powered by human energy or fossil fuels is limited by distance, yet terrestrial vehicles are agile (successfully accommodating the individual yearning for movement). Aeronautical vehicles possess great speed and may travel great distance, yet airplanes and their brethren represent collective movement and/or rarified flight path (i.e. commercial airlines and space shuttle exploration respectively). When the qualities of land-based and air-based vehicles merge, fueled by alternative energy sources, the skycar is born.

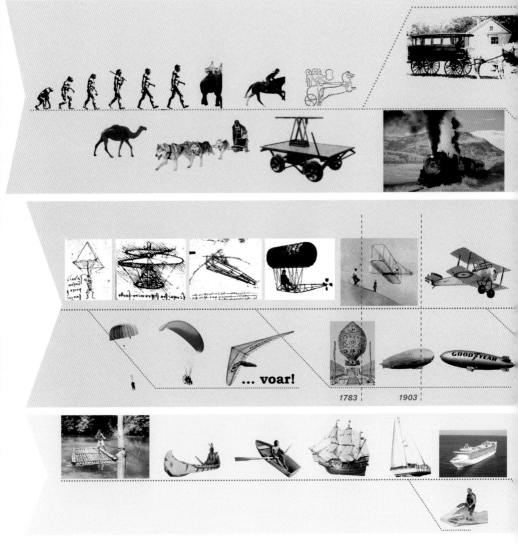

... voar!

1783   1903

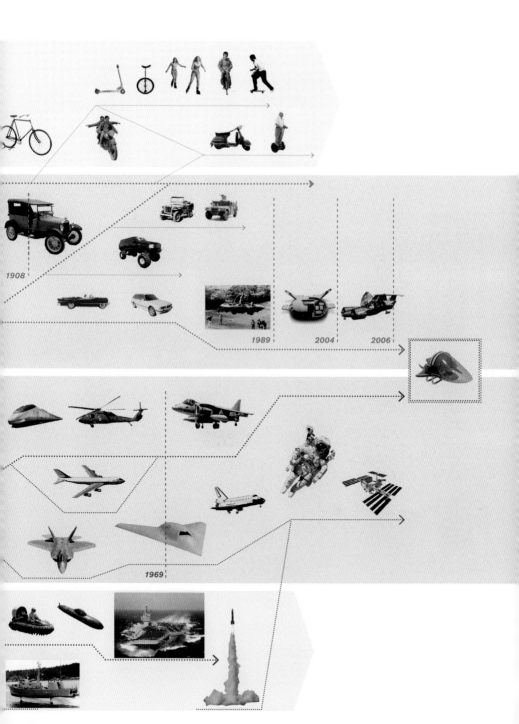

1908

1989

2004

2006

1969

CAR EVOLUTION DIAGRAM / CAR TO SKYCAR: Transition of the Vehicle

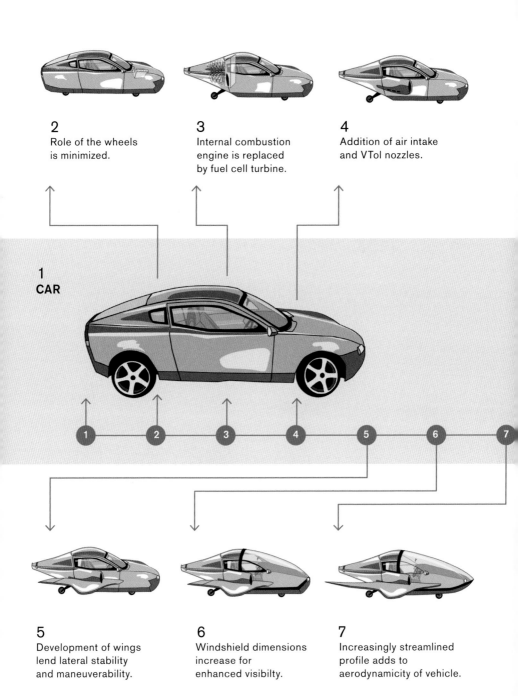

2
Role of the wheels
is minimized.

3
Internal combustion
engine is replaced
by fuel cell turbine.

4
Addition of air intake
and VTol nozzles.

1
CAR

5
Development of wings
lend lateral stability
and maneuverability.

6
Windshield dimensions
increase for
enhanced visibilty.

7
Increasingly streamlined
profile adds to
aerodynamicity of vehicle.

FINAL SKYCAR TYPOLOGY

How can we imagine the evolution of the skycar? Among the basic physical differences between terrestrial cars and skycars, the notions of energy and speed present the greatest disparities. Skycars' energy derives from fuel cell technology (rather than from fossil fuel consumption), offering an optimistic commentary on a future environment. Skycars' aeronautical shape, inherent speed, and subsequent reduction in travel time, radically transform our perception of space and distance.

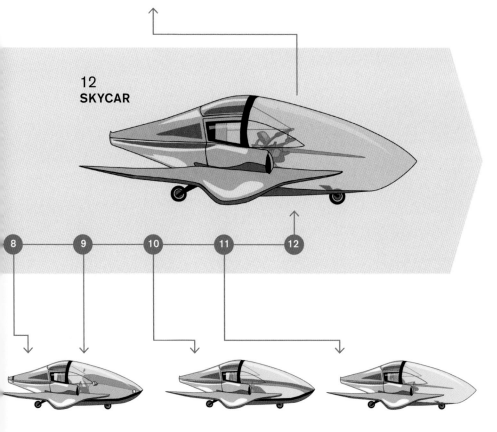

12
SKYCAR

8 — 9 — 10 — 11 — 12

8+9
Steering wheel replaced by 3-d joystick controls. Removal of dashboard allows improved views of traffic below.

10
Computer navigation and heads-up display replace conventional headlights and rear-view mirrors.

11
Removal of other frontal elements to maximize 360° visibility.

CATALOG

THE SKYCAR COLLECTION

How does the automobile of today evolve into the skycar of tomorrow?

The technological differences between the terrestrial car and the skycar are significant, yet skycar technology already exists today in several different vehicles and emerging projects.

This catalog is a collection of yet unrealized skycars, their exact characteristics based entirely in existing technology.

Barnacle
SERIES

ATtach / DEtach:
Mobile Program for
the ever-mutable city.

This vehicle series is considered a piece of moving program. Speeds are slow and movement is methodical, more vertical than horizontal. The Barnacle uses "magnetic linking" capabilities as its only means of connection. Large turbines function much like the blades of a helicopter, producing the necessary lift and propulsion. Seating can be arranged to promote social interaction, or removed completely for a floating dance club, which could re-attach to building infrastructure at will.

Barnacle Series Models

Sport

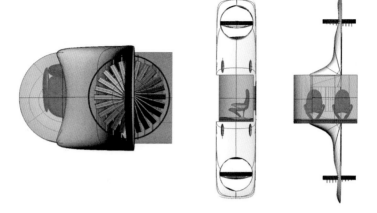

Family

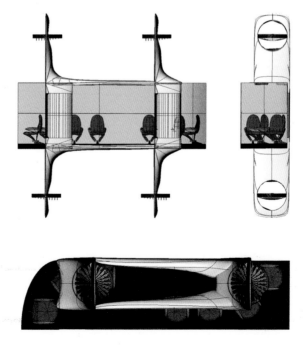

Mass Transit

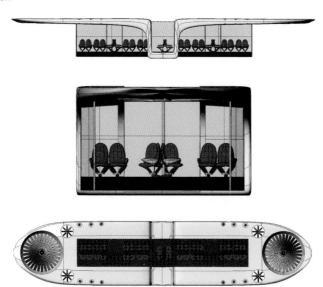

Utility

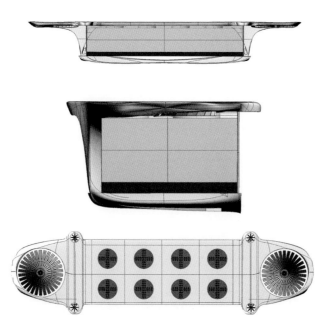

Barnacle Series Specs

1: Pod Shape

The general form
is established to
facilitate the function
of the vehicle.

2: Sociopetal Seating

Seating is inserted in
configurations based
on program type.

3: Vertical Bias

Engines are connected
and pushed to the sides to
avoid obscuring the upward
view of the passengers
and to maintain hovering
capabilities.

4: Parking Method

The armature of the vehicle
facilitates docking via
magnetic links. The volume
is free to disengage from
the armature and sit in the
building.

5: Magnetic Bumpers

Magnetic bumpers are
included as anti-collision
devices.

6: Secondary Energy Source

Solar panels are added
to the skylights on the
vehicle's roof and provide
a supplemental energy
source. The rotors can
also be configured into a
vertical position and used
to generate wind energy
when the vehicle is idle.

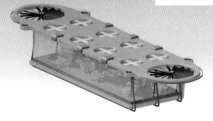

Barnacle Series 360°

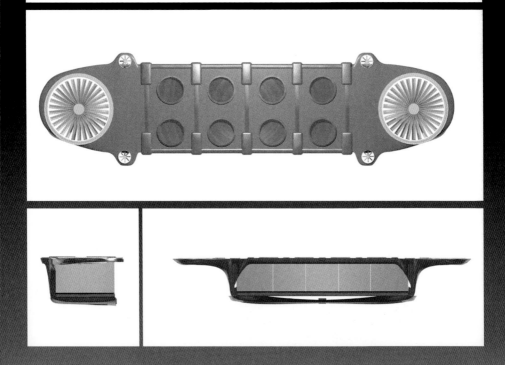

Sedan

SERIES

This vehicle series is most similar to current vehicular standards, a car that balances safety, performance, overall quality, and cost. The vehicle uses turbines for lift and propulsion. It offers multiple parking methods (both peg/prong and landing), as well as enhanced safety features such as magnetic bumpers alongside and above the vehicle. Seating in this vehicle is changeable, both forward facing and a more social, inward facing seating is possible for recreation and cruising.

Dependability, quality, and reliability...
THE most well-rounded in its class.

Sedan Series Models

Sport

Family

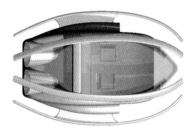

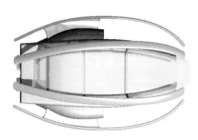

Mass Transit

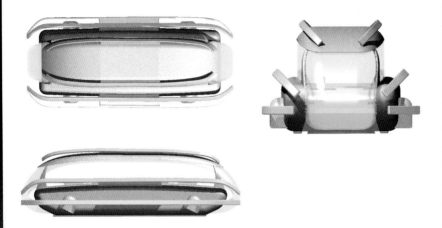

Utility

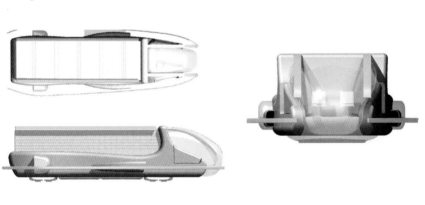

Sedan Series Specs

1: **Pod Shape**

The form is devised to accommodate both speed and comfort equally. An all-purpose form is created.

2: **Sociopetal Seating**

Seating is added in a configuration that can face forward for exterior views or to face inward to facilitate more group interaction.

3: **Vertical Bias**

The rear engine suggests predominantly horizontal movement. The force created by the turbine can also be ducted to the bottom of the vehicle for flat vertical movement.

4: **Parking Method**

Located on the bottom of the vehicle is a receptor that connects to a peg that protrudes from the building. The vehicle may also sit to park.

5: **Magnetic Bumpers**

Magnetic bumpers are implemented to prevent collisions from all angles.

6: **Secondary Energy Source**

Solar glass and air intakes harness light and wind as supplemental energy sources.

7: **Swarming *(added feature)**

Swarming is available on these vehicles via magnetic bumpers.

Transit
SERIES

Ride with us!
It's never been easier, faster or more comfortable.

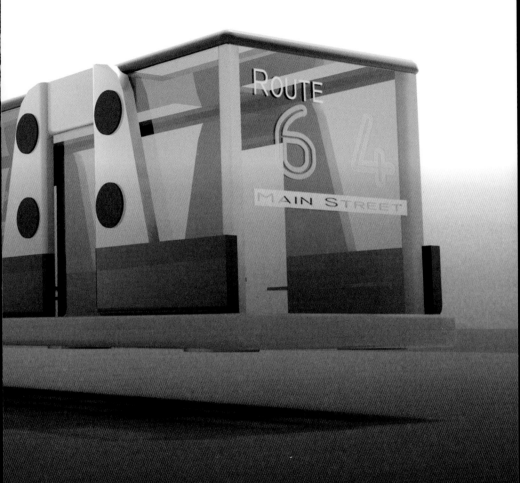

This vehicle series explores the idea of mass transit. Using flight and magnetic linking, the vehicle streamlines the inefficiencies of mass transit, particularly the act of transferring routes through entry and exiting. The bus uses turbines to create lift and propulsion, similar to the movements of the current day Harrier Jet.

Magnetic linking technology allows this bus to dock at program entrances and also allows for in-air transfers as two buses' air routes become tangential. Protected from the elements, passengers may enter the transit vehicle and switch routes without dismounting until arrival at their final destination.

Transit Series Models

Sport

Family

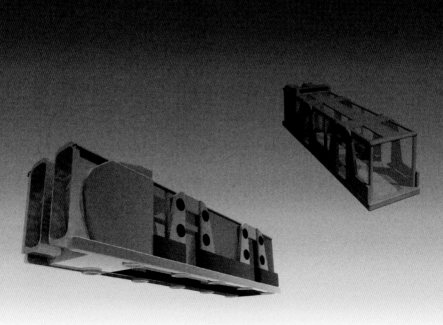

Mass Transit

Utility

Transit Series Specs

1: Pod Shape

The shape of the pod is box-like to maximize head room, allowing a high occupancy capacity.

2: Sociopetal Seating

Seating is placed around the perimeter to allow circulation and standing room in the center of bus.

3: Forward Bias

Large forward-oriented, rear engine suggests directionality with subordinate thrusters underneath to accommodate the large weight loads and maintain hovering capabilities.

4: Magnetic Docking

Air connections through the use of magnets, allow the bus to attach to the side of buildings, similar to the workings of the Barnacle series.

5: Magnetic Bumpers

Magnetic bumpers provide a safety zone between vehicles to prevent collisions.

6: Secondary Energy Source

Solar panels are embedded in the ceiling glass for supplemental solar energy. Large air intakes allow air friction to generate static electricity that may power the vehicle's peripheral systems.

Transit Series Specs

7: **Swarming**

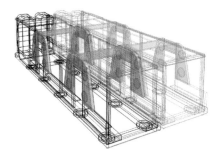

The same elements used for docking allow for buses to connect in mid-air and swarm together laterally.

Transit Series 360°

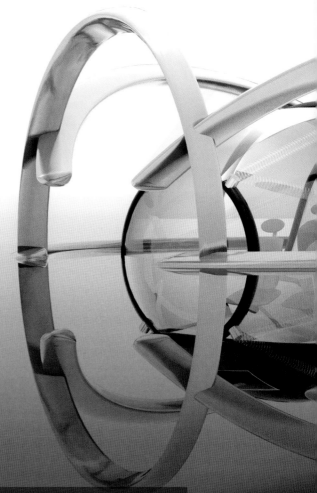

Advanced technology gives you greater control. Safety has never been more sexy.

This vehicle series prioritizes
safety above all other factors.
The passenger pod is surrounded
by a frame of magnetic bumper
technology and is suspended
in a shock-mount for additional

accident prevention. Turbines on
swivels located at the back of the
vehicle provide lift and movement.
All parking options are available.
Seating is positioned in its most
safe condition, forward facing.

Safety Series Models

Sport

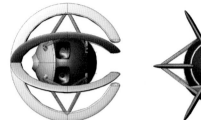  

Shock-mount Bumper Technology

Safety Series Models

Family

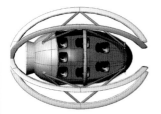

Safety Series Specs

1: Pod Shape

The form is devised to accommodate both speed and comfort equally. A generic all-purpose form is created.

2: **Directional Seating**

Seating is oriented in the direction of travel for safety and restraint systems to most efficiently handle inflight stresses experienced by the passenger.

3: **Forward Bias**

The rear engine suggests a predominantly horizontal movement. The force created by the turbine can also be ducted to the bottom of the vehicle to provide flat vertical movement.

4: Parking Method

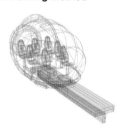

Located on the bottom of the vehicle is a receptor that connects to a peg that protrudes from the building.

5: **Magnetic Bumpers**

Magnetic bumpers prevent collisions from all angles.

6: **Secondary Energy Source**

Solar glass and air intakes are added to harness wind and light as supplemental energy sources.

7: **Swarming *(added feature)**

Swarming is available on these vehicles via magnetic bumpers.

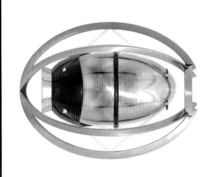

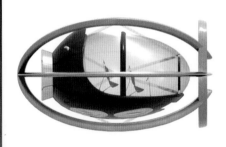

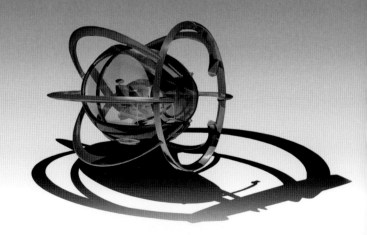

Speed
SERIES

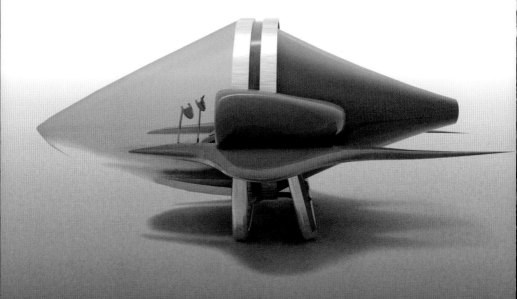

THE nimble bullet of
**precision, power,
and performance.**

This vehicle series is designed for speed, a kind of "sport" skycar. The pod shape is streamlined and seating limited to forward facing. Large turbines create increased speed and downward facing nozzles produce lift. Wings offer greater stability, control, and lift generation at high speeds. This series parks only through landing

Speed Series Models

Sport

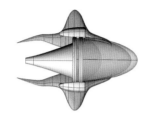

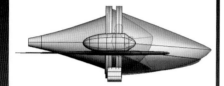

Family

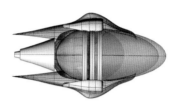

Mass Transit

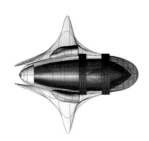

Utility

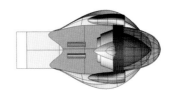

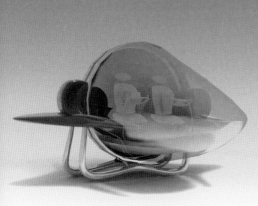

Speed Series Specs

1: Pod Shape

The shape of the pod is bullet-like to provide aerodynamic form to maximize top speed.

2: Directional Seating

Seating is forward-facing due to higher speeds and greater banking angles.

3: Forward Bias

Engines placed in the rear suggest extreme forward movement at fast speeds. This vehicle climbs and dives.

4: Parking Method

Small perches on the car's bottom allow the car to sit on a level surface.

5: Magnetic Bumpers

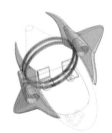

Magnetic bumpers are implemented to prevent collisions from all angles.

6: Supplemental Energy

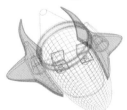

Photovoltaic panels are embedded in the ceiling glass and air resistance over the wings can be turned into usable energy.

Speed Series 360°

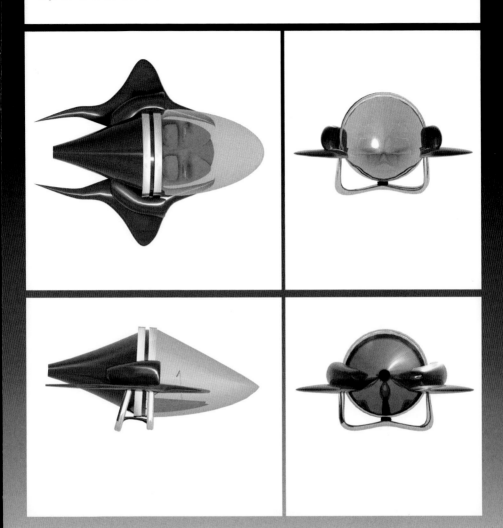

Ultimate Car

For everything you've ever wanted in a skycar...

Never sacrifice your soul.

This vehicle series tries to capture all the important qualities of the other vehicles. Movement is omni-directional through a spherical pod shape that swivels like a gyroscope within an armature containing the lift and propulsion turbines. Rings surrounding the pod offer both a flat profile to generate lift at high speeds and

an expanded option as magnetic bumpers for safety. All parking options are available, as well as the ability to link vehicles into chains to accommodate any number of passengers. This linking option is specific to this vehicle and offers increased inflight efficiency.

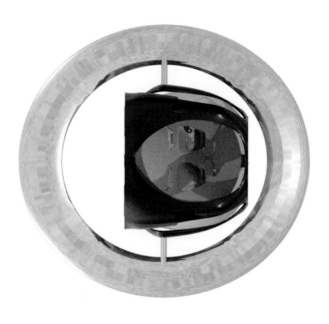

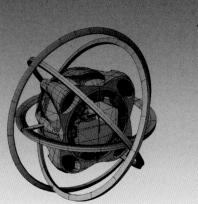

Ultimates Car Series Specs

1: Pod Shape

The shape of the pod is spherical to convey neutrality of direction and an even surface upon which to make ensuing articulations.

2: Multi-Position Seating

Seating is flexible and can be arranged into any of the availible configurations.

3: Bias-Free Propulsion

Engines are located within an armature that rotates around a self-leveling pod, providing thrust in all directions.

4: Landing Method

The Ultimate car is compatible with all three parking methods: magnetic docking, prong parking, and sitting.

5: Magnetic Bumpers & Active Evasion

A series of rings surrounding the car form a protective cage of magnetic bumper similar to those on the Safety Series car. Alternatively, the rings may be used in unison to actively navigate around potential danger.

6: Swarming

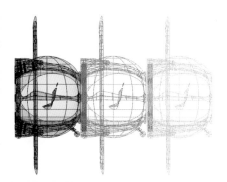

The magnetic docking unit also allows this vehicle to link together in chains for flexibility of use and transportation efficiency. Additionally, the magnetic bumpers facilitate swarming formations.

SkyBike
& SkyVespa
SERIES

This vehicle series is designed for one or two-person transport. Its form is derived for maximum power, speed, distance, and comfort. Used as a cruising vehicle, the skybike's primary turbine engine produces high pick-up rate. A rudder at the skybike's tail allows for maneuverability. Horizontal and vertical fins control steering and lift direction.
An alternate to the skybike is the skyVespa. The skyVespa is more compact, better for stop and go traffic, short distances and lower speeds.

**May the wind be
at your back!**

SkyVespa Series 360°

SkyBike Series Specs

1: **Frame Shape**

The sleek shape of the bike is designed to ensure aerodynamic performance along with a fast and aggressive appearance.

2: **Seating**

The seats are adapted from a typical two passenger motorcycle.

3: **Engine**

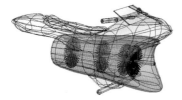 

The turbine engine is the primary component of the bike, emphasizing fast, forward movement. A series of side-nozzles offer hovering capabilities and assist lateral balance.

4: **Parking**

A small, low-profile stand is located on the bottom of the bike, allowing the bike to stand alone while the engines are off.

5: **Maneuvering**

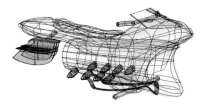

A sky-rudder is incorporated to give the bike maneuvering capabilities.

5: **Rudder**

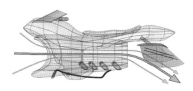

Horizontal fins rotate vertically to control steering in the vertical direction.

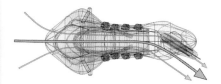

Vertical fins rotate horizontally to direct air left or right, allowing the bike to turn.

SKYCAR TAXONOMY: A Summary

SIZE (passengers + function)
Skycar designs are divided into 4 typological categories analogos to freight vehicles, buses, 7 passenger cars and 2 passenger cars to create a variety of functions and options. How does the size of a vehicle affect the implementation of other systems? Are certain technologies invalid beyond certain dimensions?

COLLISION PREVENTION
(evasion vs. magnetic bumpers) How do skycars avoid collisions? Evasion capability enabled by ailerons provides quicker maneuverability. Alternately, magnetic bumpers may prevent skycars from touching one another.

SPEED (velocity + aerodynamics) Speed affects turning radii, the ability to create lift, and the ability to maneuver. How does a city respond to differences in speed? How fast does a skycar need to be? How does the experience of the city change?

SKYCAR TAXONOMY The objective of the skycar taxonomy was to investigate a wide range of possible vehicle types, given a limited and inevitable exhaustion of fossil fuel. The seven parameters that guided the design of vehicles are arranged into a matrix. Six types of vehicles were designed, including a comprehensive (ultimate) vehicle.

size

directional bias

speed+aerodynamics

PME hydrogen fuel cell

seating arrangement

collision prevention

swarming capability

parking method

size

directional bias

speed+aerodynamics

PME hydrogen fuel cell

seating arrangement

collision prevention

swarming capability

parking method

SUPPLEMENTAL ENERGY
Air friction, solar power, and wind power are options by which the skycar can gain additional energy to run peripherals when in operation or to feed energy into the building when parked. How will the supplemental energy systems look?

SEATING ARRANGE-MENT (Sociopetal, sociofugal, or directional) Given that the skycar will be largely computer-automated, no longer demanding a driver's rapt attention, what is the favorable seating position given each car's use?

SWARMING CAPABILITY (individual vs. collective) Can automated navigational systems, swarming, or increased aerodynamic efficiency create opportunities for individual transport to transform into collective transport?

PARKING (Docking vs. Linking vs. sitting) How does the car park? Does it dock? Does it link to a structure via peg or prong? Does it sit or land on a platform?

The skycar designs were the first steps toward producing a hypothetical city. The vehicle properties generated the shape and form of the pathway network, integral to city form, and also the parking strategies, and the interface between pathways and program.

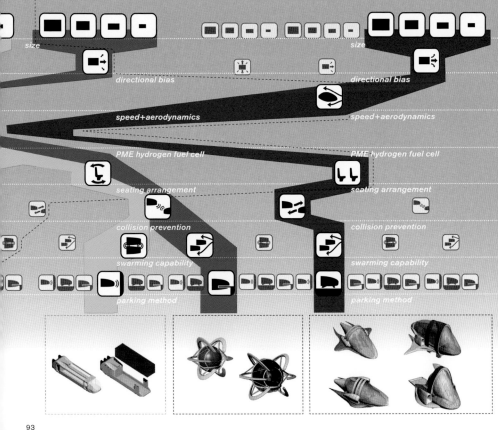

THE MAKING OF SKYCAR CITY: THE 5 M CITY

PROGRAM

As the development of cities tends toward a recursive nature, the position of program and its relation to infrastructure is an initial starting point to hypothesize about future urban forms. When land (destinations/ place/program) or infrastructure (roads/path/movement) develops, these essential components of the city influence each other in a seemingly simultaneous fashion. In order to define the relationship between the two –and perhaps to circumvent indecision based on infinite questions of recursion– certain parameters establish a base for the generation of program distribution.

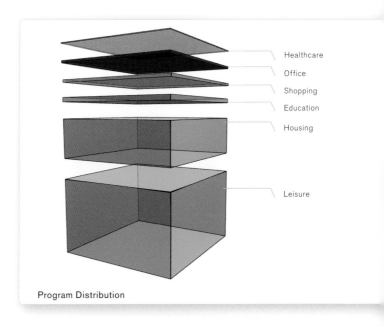

Healthcare

Office

Shopping

Education

Housing

Leisure

Program Distribution

THE 5M CITY

Study city set at five million residents: In barely a century, the largest city in the world first surpassed a population of five million inhabitants. In 1900, London was the largest city on earth, with 6.48 million residents, and New York City the second, with roughly 4.2 million. While a relatively new phenomenon, urban centers have experienced unprecedented population growth over the course of the last century. In 2000, Tokyo-Yokohama was the largest city in the world with a population topping 33 million people. There are now at least 25 cities with a population greater than 10 million.

In 2006, these "Cities of Five Million" appear often and throughout the globe.

More than in the past, these high-density cities are now common. Roughly 38 metropolitan areas worldwide have populations between 5 to 9.9 million; furthermore, an additional 60 metropolitan areas maintain populations between 3 and 4.9 million. As the following pages illustrate, a city of this size requires tremendous resources and space. Its increasing frequency substantiates, if not demands, a closer investigation.

The notion of upward, or vertical movement offers significant possibilities for densification, a prerequisite for increasing a city's efficiency and enhancing its response to population growth. It also begs the following questions: In a city where a location fifty stories off the ground can be accessed just as easily as the ground floor, what factors determine program location? New forms of accessibility no longer mandate that such programs as office or living space are best situated high above, or that public spaces such as parks need to remain at grade. How many and what type of program/destinations are required to support 5,000,000 inhabitants? What are the major programmatic nodes? Could the very definition of such nodes be challenged—where the concept of node and path, program and infrastructure, become more closely joined?

Year 2000: Cities with a population of greater than 5,000,000 but less than 6,000,000 inhabitants...

CITY	POPULATION
Lahore	5,920,000
Boston	5,815,000
Dallas-Ft Worth	5,785,000
Kinshasa	5,750,000
Bangalore	5,687,000
Johannesburg	5,530,000
Toronto	5,470,000
Detroit	5,415,000
St. Petersburg	5,410,000
Baghdad	5,400,000
Madrid	5,300,000
Miami	5,289,000
Houston	5,176,000

Since 2000, Cities whose populations have grown to 5-6 million residents...

CITY	POPULATION
Philadelphia	5,922,000
Rhine-Ruhr	5,823,000
Belo Horizonte	5,588,000
Hyderabad	5,534,000
Wuhan	5,169,000

PROGRAMMATIC VOLUME ESTIMATES

MVRDV's recent book, KM3, offers research on programmatic volume requirements necessary to support a city of 1 million people. This data serves as a basis for the subsequent development of Skycar City. The following chart represents this information and was adjusted to accommodate Skycar City's larger size at 5 million.

POPULATION			
	population	1,000,000.00	people
	% of population in work	44.00	%
	working population	440,000.00	people
	% of working population in primary employment	4.00	%
	working population in primary employment	17,600.00	people
	% of working population in secondary employment	22.00	%
	working population in secondary employment	96,800.00	people
	% of working population in tertiary employment	74.00	%
	working population in tertiary employment	325,600.00	people
HOUSING			
	average family size	2.31	people
	number of households	432,900.43	families
	average home area	125.00	m²
	total home area	54,112,534.11	m²
	height	3.00	m
	average home volume	375.00	m³
	total home volume	162,337,662.24	m³
OFFICE			
	total office units (1 person)	3,256,000.00	quantity
	average office area	9.50	m²
	total office area	3,093,200.00	m²
	height	3.00	m
	average office volume	28.50	m³
	total office volume	9,279,600.00	m³
EDUCATION			
	% of total population in education	19.86	%
	total students in education	198,600.00	people
.Primary			
	% of students in primary education	49.24	%
	total students in primary education	97,790.00	people
	student populaton per school	439.07	people
	total primary education schools	452.00	quantity
	area per primary education school	5,895.00	m²
	total primary education school area	2,666,414.77	m²
	height	4.00	m
	volume per primary education school	23,580.00	m³
	total primary education school volume	10,665,659.00	m³
.Secondary			
	% of students in secondary education	27.91	%
	total students in secondary education	55,429.00	people
	student population count per school	4,771.77	people
	total secondary education schools	42.00	quantity
	area per secondary education school	28,873.00	m²
	total secondary education school area	1,201,687.30	m²
	height	4.00	m
	volume per secondary education school	115,492.00	m³
	total secondary education school volume	4,806,749.19	m³

.Vocational Secondary	% of students in vocational secondary education	9.63	%
	total students in vocational secondary education	19,125.18	people
	student populaton count per school	40,743.59	people
	total vocational secondary education schools	5.00	quantity
	area per vocational secondary education school	78,161.00	m²
	total vocational secondary education school area	380,986.91	m²
	height	4.00	m
	volume per vocational secondary education school	312,644.00	m³
	total vocational secondary education school volume	1,523,947.00	m³
.Vocational	% of students in vocational education	0.09	%
	total students in vocational education	17,059.00	people
	student populaton per school	48,892.31	people
	total vocational education schools	4.00	quantity
	area per vocational education school	82,504.00	m²
	total vocational education school area	335,130.30	m²
	height	4.00	m
	volume per vocational education school	330,016.00	m³
	total vocational education school volume	1,340,521.19	m³
.University	% of students in university level education	4.63	%
	total students in university level education	9,195.18	people
	student population per university	244,461.50	people
	total unversities	1.00	quantity
	area per university	282,692.00	m²
	total university area	22,658.38	m²
	height	4.00	m
	volume per university	918,633.51	m³
	total university volume	746,295.90	m³
	total educational facilities	504.00	quantity
	total educational area	4,813,877.66	m²
	total educational volume	19,083,173.02	m³
HOSPITAL	population count per general hospital	111,982.10	people
	number of general hospitals	9.00	quantity
	average number of beds per hospital	57,825.00	quantity
	average area per general hospital	2,457.56	m²
	total area of general hospital	21,946.01	m²
	height	4.00	m
	average volume per general hospital	9,830.24	m³
	total volume of general hospital	87,784.03	m³
PARKING	cars per person	0.33	quantity
	total number of cars	333,333.33	quantity
	parking area per car	13.75	m²
	total parking area	4,583,333.33	m²
	height	2.50	m
	parking volume per car	34.38	m³
	total parking volume	11,458,333.33	m³
AGRICULTURE	total number of farms	5.75	quantity
	total farm area	1,216,026,000.11	m²
	total farm volume	6,435,571,000.65	m³

INDUSTRY	total number of industrial enterprises	856.13	quantity
	total industry area	4,493,804.12	m²
	total industry volume	59,205,639.09	m³
	total industry volume with buffer	18,889,314,154.90	m³

SHOP	total number of stores	5,884.00	quantity
	total area of stores	2,681,262.64	m²
	total volume of stores	10,725,050.58	m³

LEISURE	extra small leisure facilities	3,888.00	quantity
.X-Small Leisure	population count per extra small hard leisure facility	271.30	people
..hard surface	extra small hard surface	3,686.00	quantity
	arverage area per hard surface	475.03	m²
	total area of hard surface facility	1,750,960.77	m²
	average height	5.00	m
	average volume of hard surface facility	2,375.15	m³
	total volume of hard surface	8,754,803.86	m³
..grass surface	population count per extra small grass leisure facility	5,154.64	people
	extra small grass surface	194.00	quantity
	arverage area per grass surface	782.92	m²
	total area of grass surface facility	151,886.49	m²
	average height	6.00	m
	average volume of grass surface facility	4,697.52	m³
	total volume of grass surface	911,318.91	m³
..snow/ ice	population count per extra small snow/ice leisure facility	250,000.00	people
	extra small snow/ice surface	4.00	quantity
	arverage area per snow/ice surface	1,224.00	m²
	total area of snow/ice surface facility	4,896.00	m²
	average height	6.00	m
	average volume of snow/ice surface facility	7,344.00	m³
	total volume of snow/ice surface	23,376.00	m³
..water	population count per extra small water leisure facility	250,000.00	people
	extra small water surface	4.00	quantity
	arverage area per water surface	726.85	m²
	total area of water surface facility	2,907.38	m²
	average height	11.00	m
	average volume of water surface facility	7,995.30	m³
	total volume of water surface	31,981.18	m³
.Smalll Leisure	small leisure facilities	715.00	quantity
..hard surface	population count per small hard leisure facility	1,976.29	people
	small hard surface	506.00	quantity
	arverage area per hard surface	5,524.50	m²
	total area of hard surface facility	2,795,397.51	m²
	average height	7.00	m
	average volume of hard surface facility	38,671.52	m³
	total volume of hard surface	19,576,782.59	m³
..grass surface	population count per small grass leisure facility	18,181.82	people
	small grass surface	55.00	quantity
	arverage area per grass surface	4,156.00	m²
	total area of grass surface facility	228,579.98	m²

	average height	6.00	m
	average volume of grass surface facility	24,936.00	m³
	total volume of grass surface	1,371,479.86	m³
..snow surface	population count per small snow/ice leisure facility	6,493.61	people
	small snow/ice surface	154.00	quantity
	arverage area per snow/ice surface	2,290.00	m²
	total area of snow/ice surface facility	352,660.03	m²
	average height	12.00	m
	average volume of snow/ice surface facility	27,480.00	m³
	total volume of snow/ice surface	4,231,920.32	m³
.Medium Leisure	medium leisure facilities	405.00	quantity
..hard surface	population count per medium hard leisure facility	20,000.00	people
	medium hard surface	50.00	quantity
	arverage area per hard surface	16,688.04	m²
	total area of hard surface facility	833,402.08	m²
	average height	15.00	m
	average volume of hard surface facility	250,020.63	m³
	total volume of hard surface	12,501,031.25	m³
..grass surface	population count per medium grass leisure facility	2,967.36	people
	medium grass surface	337.00	quantity
	arverage area per grass surface	25,048.40	m²
	total area of grass surface facility	8,441,310.94	m²
	average height	13.00	m
	average volume of grass surface facility	325,629.20	m³
	total volume of grass surface	109,737,042.27	m³
..snow / ice	population count per medium snow/ice leisure facility	125,000.00	people
	medium snow/ice surface	8.00	quantity
	average area per snow/ice surface	133,250.00	m²
	total area of snow/ice surface facility	1,066,000.00	m²
	average height	4.00	m
	average volume of snow/ice surface facility	533,000.00	m³
	total volume of snow/ice surface	4,264,000.00	m³
..water	population count per medium water leisure facility	100,000.00	people
	medium water surface	10.00	quantity
	arverage area per water surface	27,566.00	m²
	total area of water surface facility	275,660.00	m²
	average height	9.00	m
	average volume of water surface facility	248,094.00	m³
	total volume of water surface	2,480,940.00	m³
.Large Leisure	large leisure facilities	23.00	quantity
..hard surface	population count per large hard leisure facility	142,857.10	people
	large hard surface	7.00	quantity
	arverage area per hard surface	110,304.00	m²
	total area of hard surface facility	772,128.23	m²
	average height	14.00	m
	average volume of hard surface facility	1,544,256.00	m³
	total volume of hard surface	10,809,795.24	m³
..grass surface	population count per large grass leisure facility	125,000.00	people
	large grass surface	8.00	quantity

..grass surface	average area per grass surface	242,653.13	m²
	total area of grass surface facility	1,941,225.00	m²
	average height	7.00	m
	average volume of grass surface facility	1,698,571.88	m³
	total volume of grass surface	13,588,575.00	m³
	population count per large water leisure facility	125,000.00	people
	large water surface	8.00	quantity
..water	arverage area per water surface	177,500.00	m²
	total area of water surface facility	1,420,000.00	m²
	average height	7.00	m
	average volume of water surface facility	1,242,500.00	m³
	total volume of water surface	9,940,000.00	m³
	extra large leisure surface	31.00	quantity
	population count per extra large grass leisure facility	52,631.58	people
.X-Large Leisure	extra large grass surface	19.00	quantity
..grass leisure	arverage area per grass surface	124,419.50	m²
	total area of grass surface facility	2,363,970.45	m²
	average height	26.00	m
	average volume of grass surface facility	3,234,907.00	m³
	total volume of grass surface	61,463,231.77	m³
	population count per extra large water leisure facility	83,333.33	people
	extra large water surface	12.00	quantity
	arverage area per water surface	300,000.00	m²
..water	total area of water surface facility	3,600,000.14	m²
	average height	14.00	m
	average volume of water surface facility	4,200,000.00	m³
	total volume of water surface	50,400,092.00	m³
	total leisure facility	**5,062.00**	**quantity**
	total area of leisure facility	**25,998,077.63**	**m²**
	total volume of leisure facility	**310,051,299.09**	**m³**
ENERGY	total energy from existing system	19,357,624.99	kWh
..pv	total area of photovoltaic cells	442,003.71	m²
..turbine	total volume for 44m turbines	130,432,140.00	m³
	total number of 44m turbines	48.40	quantity
	total volume for 4m turbines	33,001,548.00	m³
	total number of 4m turbines	14,323.00	quantity
	total area for energy production	**4,003,820.49**	**m²**
	total volume for energy production	**163,875,692.79**	**m³**
WASTE	total waste volume	183,707.55	m³
WATER	water consumption per person	193.00	liters
	total water consuption	193,000,000.00	liters
	total water volume (including all water uses)	159,140,062.64	m³

FOREST	..Pine 01	area	102,000,000.00	m²
		height	40.00	m
		volume	4,080,000,000.00	m³
	..Pine 02	area	87,000,000.00	m²
		height	40.00	m
		volume	3,480,000,000.00	m³
.Forest	..Forest 01	area	43,000,000.00	m²
		height	40.00	m
		volume	1,720,000,000.00	m³
	..Forest 02	area	52,000,000.00	m²
		height	40.00	m
		volume	2,080,000,000.00	m³
.Sub-Tropic	..Tropic 01	area	49,000,000.00	m²
		height	100.00	m
		volume	4,900,000,000.00	m³
	..Tropic 02	area	15,000,000.00	m²
		height	100.00	m
		volume	1,500,000,000.00	m³
.Mosses		area	94,000,000.00	m²
		height	20.00	m
		volume	680,000,000.00	m³
	total forest area		**427,000,000.00**	**m²**
	total forest volume		**17,840,000,000.003,888.00**	**m³**

From the previous statistics, a volumetric estimate for the needs of 5,000,000 people measured in cubic meters:

HOUSING - - - - - - - - - - - - - - - - - 811,688,311.7
OFFICE - - - - - - - - - - - - - - - - - - 46,398,000.0
EDUCATION- - - - - - - - - - - - - - - -95,415,865.3
HEALTH CARE - - - - - - - - - - - - - - 15,384,843.6
INDUSTRY - - - - - - - - - - - - - - - - -296,028,195.5
SHOPPING - - - - - - - - - - - - - - - - 53,625,252.9
LEISURE - - - - - - - - - - - - - - - - 1,550,256,495.4
WASTE MANAGEMENT- - - - - - - - - - - 918,537.7
ENERGY PRODUCTION - - - - - - -819,378,463.9
WATER - - - - - - - - - - - - - - - - - -795,700,313.2
FORREST - - - - - - - - - - - - - 89,200,000,000.0
AGRICULTURE- - - - - - - - - - - -32,177,850,000.0

These programmatic volumes will become the basic building blocks for determining where things are in our hypothetical city.

PROGRAM ARRANGEMENT / 3 Options

In a typical city, program is arranged two dimensionally across the ground plane on a grid system or other type of organizational network. Having broken the elevator's monopoly on vertical access, the skycar liberates the city, allowing it to appropriate the space above. However, this escape from the surface grid does not eliminate the need for organization. Common existing city arrangements offer conceptual models for exploring large scale programmatic relationships, which are defined as forest, agriculture, industry, and urban program. For the purposes of this discussion, the fine grained program readily available in a city was grouped as one type, the "urban program."

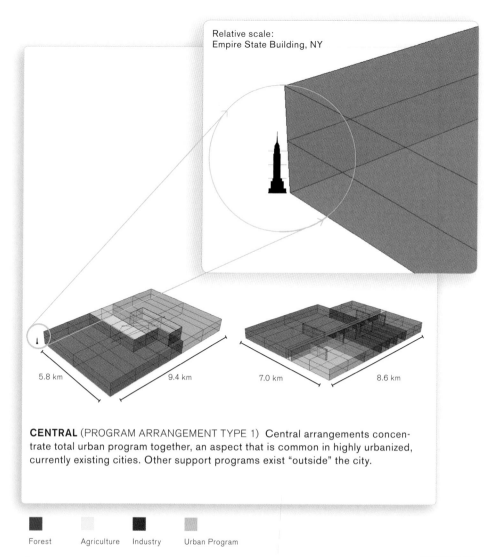

Relative scale:
Empire State Building, NY

5.8 km 9.4 km 7.0 km 8.6 km

CENTRAL (PROGRAM ARRANGEMENT TYPE 1) Central arrangements concentrate total urban program together, an aspect that is common in highly urbanized, currently existing cities. Other support programs exist "outside" the city.

Forest   Agriculture   Industry   Urban Program

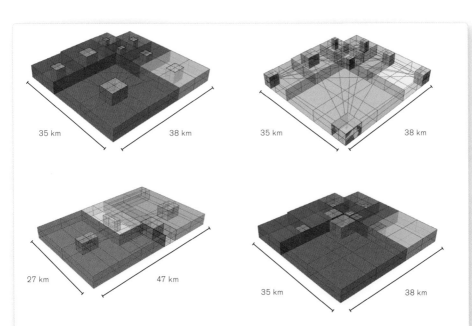

35 km   38 km   35 km   38 km

27 km   47 km

35 km   38 km

DISTRICT (PROGRAM ARRANGEMENT TYPE 2) District arrangements separate total urban program into several smaller segments, offering greater flexibility in the creation various programmatic adjacencies. Residency is determined by choice: Simple personal preference or occupational convenience may influence the settling pattern of several different districts that maintain distinct identities.

BORDER (PROGRAM ARRANGEMENT TYPE 3)
The Border arrangement distributes total urban program along the edge of other programs. This arrangement would expose the greatest amount of surface area for the urban program and like the Central arrangement, would allow other program-matic areas to remain pure, excluding the insertion of city program.

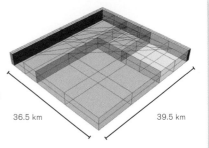

36.5 km   39.5 km

PROGRAM ARRANGEMENT / Building Placement

The placement of built form in District City and Central City suggests a comparison between dispersed and concentrated program models. For the purposes of a skycar driven city, the factor of distance between downtown functions is minimized, based on an assumption of the skycar's tremendous velocity. At 150 kmh, for example, distances between program components do not wholly determine idealized scenarios. Rather, other factors such as access to natural light and air suggest qualitative differences within various program placement options. As travel time (commuting distances) diminish as an issue, the potential for an "ultimate city" development of 20 million inhabitants emerges as an amalgamation of mega-districts (fully comprised of urban program). Massive and/or specialized components of program such as forest or agriculture may exist separately from urban program elements. Accordingly, the studio focused on the development of the urban program, as rendered in the downtown area of Central City.

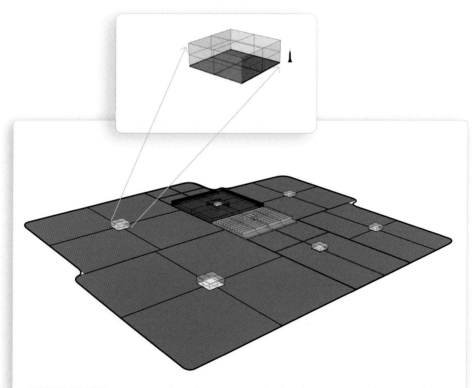

DISTRICT CITY appears, at first glance, more suburban in nature, creating potential for distinct programs to be coordinated with specific purposes (i.e. worker housing near industry, farm buildings near agriculture, etc.). Pathways are much longer between elements of program, yet the program distribution within each district remains the same, but at a reduced scale.

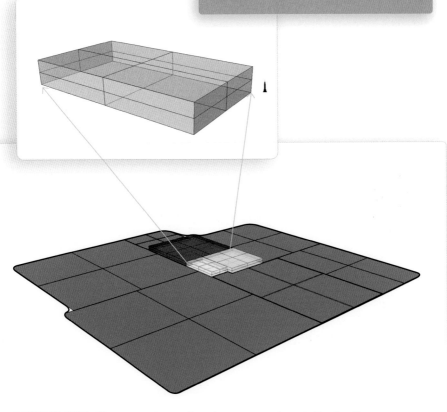

Of the three Program Arrangement Types (Central, District, and Border), further program distribution investigations were conducted on the Central and District Types.

CENTRAL CITY offers a conglomeration of program and proximity of pathways. Based partially on notions of Walter Christaller's 1933 Central Place Theory (asserting the predominance of urban centralization as a natural organizing principle), the city's program is compacted together. The program assumes an organic growth pattern radiating from the center, or downtown area.

/ **Building Placement** // Parameters

Because the arrangement of program within a highly vertical city requires a three dimensional consideration of the city's cross section, the studio established criteria for the diagrammatic positioning of program within built form. In the star-shaped diagrams, each spoke defines a parameter relevant to the placement of program, offering a ranking system that helps to locate place within the city. The importance of each parameter is ranked from lowest at the center and highest towards the ends of the spokes, offering comparative opportunity to assess program type and position.

HOUSING	LEISURE	SHOPPING
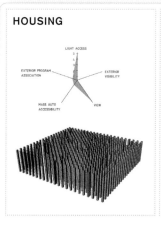	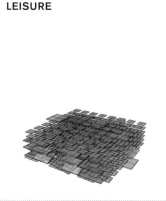	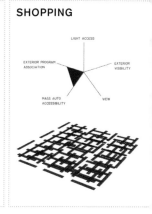

Housing is dispersed evenly across the whole city. Since every resident requires a dwelling, housing was used as "filler" to occupy the interstitial space between nodes. As housing's most fundamental parameters include access to natural light and views, housing was also positioned toward the upper part of the city and floor plates were kept relatively small.

Leisure is the only category that lacks a specific diagram because it encompasses a large variety of programmatic elements and is therefore conceived via its scale as small, medium, large, and extra-large components. Leisure program was dispersed evenly throughout the city and in some cases, depending on its scale, it is used to bridge between other areas of program and provided opportunity for flexible, site-specific configuration.

Shopping is arranged horizontally for ease of pedestrian circulation and placed in the lower levels of the city because it is less dependent on access to natural light or views.

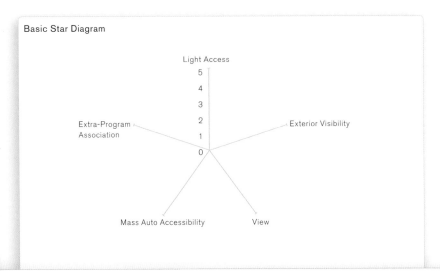

Basic Star Diagram

Light Access

Extra-Program Association

Exterior Visibility

Mass Auto Accessibility

View

EDUCATION

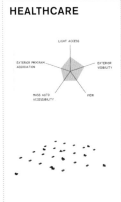

Education includes all types of schools. Elementary schools are distributed adjacent to housing to minimize travel distances for young children. High schools were fewer in number and larger in scale and positioned separately from housing. Universities were the largest in scale and given their high number of users, comprised nodes onto themselves.

HEALTHCARE

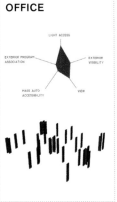

Healthcare encompasses hospitals, nursing homes or assisted living for the sick and elderly. It has a small but vital presence in the city. Nursing homes are situated to maximize natural light and fresh air. Hospitals are distributed throughout the city to ensure that no point in the city is more than a five minute ride away.

OFFICE

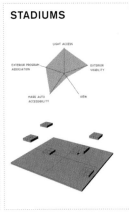

Office program is grouped into clusters and is positioned at the same level as housing. This program is based on additional considerations for mass car accessibility, which is clustered into a series of small destination areas rather evenly dispersed nodes.

STADIUMS

Stadiums and arenas are large elements that must accommodate large amounts of traffic on an irregular basis. Their primary difference is the indoor (arena) and outdoor (stadium) nature of their types, which initiated distinct locations within the city: arenas lower in the city and stadiums at more elevated heights to take advantage of natural light.

PROGRAM ARRANGEMENT / District and Central City

Based on research into general Program arrangement and building placement parameters, a specific, spatial program arrangement is generated for both the District and Central City types.

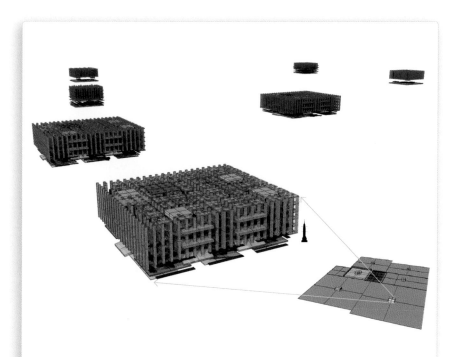

DISTRICT CITY The total program for the District City model accommodates the needs of 5 million inhabitants. The star-diagram process repeats in every district, each uniquely configured according to varying parameters and overall volumetric requirements. Additionally, the nature of the program determines its overall arrangement: (i.e. the clustering of office space or the even dispersion of housing throughout the city).

The studio focused on the Central City type for further investigation into the location of program nodes, a further level of specificifty.

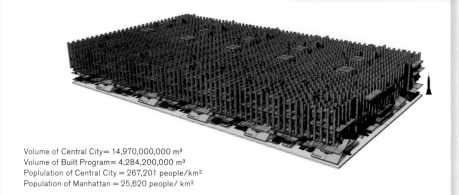

Volume of Central City= 14,970,000,000 m³
Volume of Built Program= 4,284,200,000 m³
Poplulation of Central City = 267,201 people/km²
Population of Manhattan = 25,620 people/ km²

CENTRAL CITY In the Central City model, the total program (of 5 million) is arranged into one centralized zone. The star diagram method acts again, but on a larger scale. When compared to the more programmatically dispersed District City model, the denser Central City model demonstrates enhanced ability to manage hyper-density, maintains a larger concentration of programmatic nodes, and possesses greater potential to develop a complex and multi-valent network of pathways.

PROGRAM ARRANGEMENT / Nodes

For this investigation, "node" is defined as the interstices within a city where programmatic function/destinations and movement coalesce and where a spatial locus or region may be articulated. In order to identify programmatic nodes in our city, information was gathered to identify population percentages and usage volume according to time and place. The subsequent chart identifies major programmatic destinations at different times of day. The chart represents the population percentage per time interval, the resultant number of individuals and the requisite number of commute vehicles employed in each destination.

UNIVERSITY
205,910 people daily

	Time	Percentage of People	Number of People	Number of Vehicles (1.5 people/car)
am	6:00-8:00	1.50%	4,905	3,270
	8:00-10:00	5.00%	16,350	10,900
	10:00-12:00	16.00%	52,320	34,880
pm	12:00-2:00	19.00%	62,130	41,420
	2:00-4:00	18.00%	58,860	39,240
	4:00-6:00	14.00%	45,780	30,520
	6:00-8:00	12.50%	40,875	27,250
	8:00-10:00	7.00%	22,890	15,260

HIGH SCHOOL
151,200 people daily

	Time	Percentage of People	Number of People	Number of Vehicles (2.1 people/car)
am	6:00-8:00	10.00%	33,359	15,885
	8:00-10:00	8.00%	26,687	12,708
	10:00-12:00	48.00%	160,123	76,249
pm	12:00-2:00	64.00%	213,498	101,666
	2:00-4:00	12.00%	40,031	19,062
	4:00-6:00	33.00%	110,085	52,421
	6:00-8:00	14.00%	46,703	22,239
	8:00-10:00	2.00%	6,672	3,177

OFFICE
762,810 people daily

	Time	Percentage of People	Number of People	Number of Vehicles (1.0 person/car)
am	6:00-8:00	11.00%	97,842	97,842
	8:00-10:00	53.80%	478,538	478,538
	10:00-12:00	53.80%	478,538	478,538
pm	12:00-2:00	25.00%	222,369	222,369
	2:00-4:00	53.80%	478,538	478,538
	4:00-6:00	11.00%	97,842	97,842
	6:00-8:00	35.00%	311,316	311,316
	8:00-10:00	35.00%	311,316	311,316

HOUSING
5,000,000 people daily

	Time	Percentage of People	Number of People	Number of Vehicles (1.1 people/car)
am	6:00- 8:00	11.00%	198,000	180,000
	8:00-10:00	53.80%	968,400	880,364
	10:00-12:00	53.80%	968,400	880,364
pm	12:00-2:00	25.00%	450,000	409,091
	2:00- 4:00	53.80%	968,400	880,364
	4:00-6:00	11.00%	198,000	180,000
	6:00- 8:00	35.00%	630,000	572,727
	8:00-10:00	35.00%	630,000	572,727

PROGRAM ARRANGEMENT / Node Identification

Program usage studies establish the fluctuating quantity (i.e. volume) of people traveling to each of seven major program types throughout the day. The study suggests that pathways between major program might thereby readjust as well, accommodating varying volume of traffic for peak and non-peak hours. These program/time graphs form the starting point for the programmatic organization of the city.

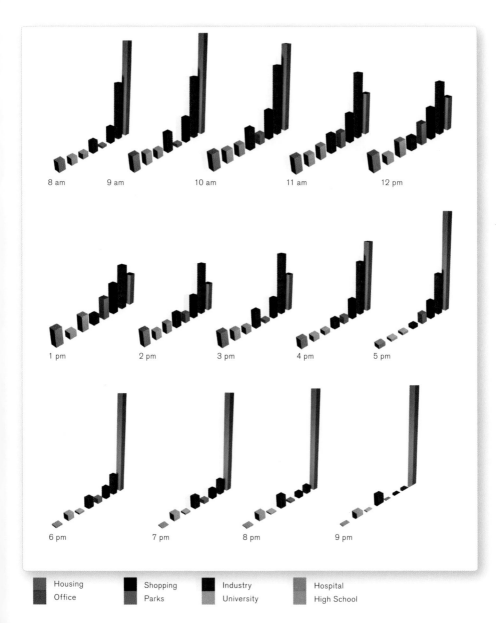

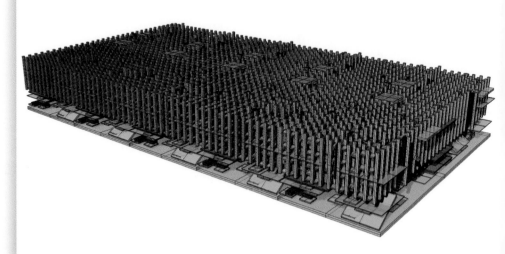

Studying the previous data and fluctuation graph informed the
selection of major and minor destinations at particular times in
our city. This information provided the raw material to designate
programmatic nodes.

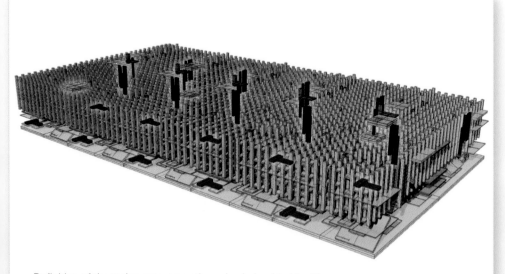

Definition of the major programmatic nodes helped to identify destination zones that would influence pathway routing and requirements for transit connections.

PATHWAYS

The relationship between pathway and programs is inherently integrated and therefore it is challenging to discuss each component independently. A description of pathways is particularly difficult as the skycar infrastructure is potentially ever-mutable and intangible; it is conceived as the empty space that unifies otherwise autonomous structures. The previous section concluded with the proposal of a conceptual programmatic framework: a potential city hovering between built precedent and the introduction of a new pathway system.

PATHWAY SYSTEMS Identifying parameters allowed for greater exploration and discovery through unanticipated results. Varied options provided a comparative framework for the selection of a pathway model. The Sputnik type was ultimately selected for further development. Its inherently nodal form is easily adaptable to a 3-D network hierarchy. Moreover, its elasticity and scalability (the ability to receive any number and size of pathways) suggests that it can facilitate, rather than impose, programmatic needs.

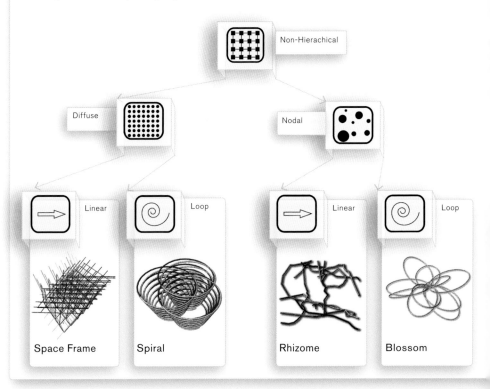

Non-Hierachical

Diffuse

Nodal

Linear

Loop

Linear

Loop

Space Frame

Spiral

Rhizome

Blossom

Developing a three-dimensional urban program in the absence of a set of working principles for a spatial organizational network necessitated the calculation of major resources (and assigned qualitative parameters) required to support a technologically advanced city. This information infrastructure informs the physical development of cities and further blurs the distinction between program and pathway due to the implicit requirements of different program types. Application of skycar paths will provide opportunities to give these concepts a form.

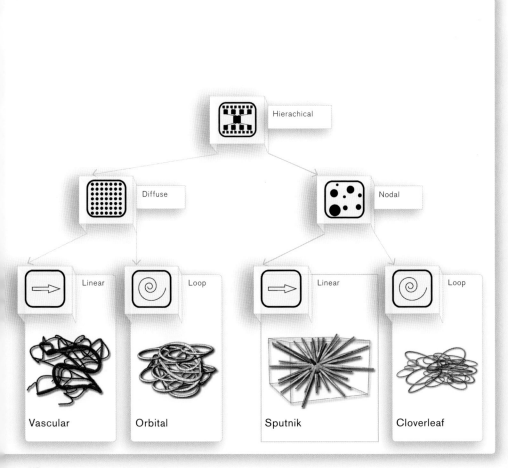

APPLICATION

By using the Sputnik system, each node functions as a "mini-sputnik" with each of its ends connected to another node. This configuration creates straight, direct connections between major destination nodes. Earlier programmatic studies identified nodes that are now applied to the new pathway system.

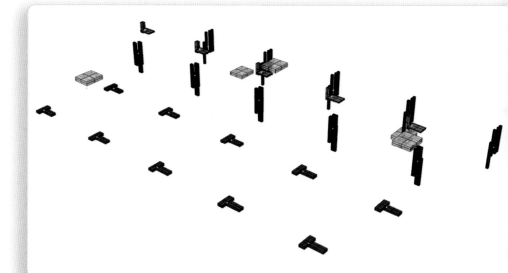

Extracted from the base program distribution, nodes interconnect via straight lines that represent the shortest possible route between destinations. This diagrammatic system forms the basis for the Sputnik model of movement. In order to convert this diagram into a set of pathways, size and dimensional factors are primary considerations that must be assessed. The following pages explore the combined influence of program and the skycar on pathway development.

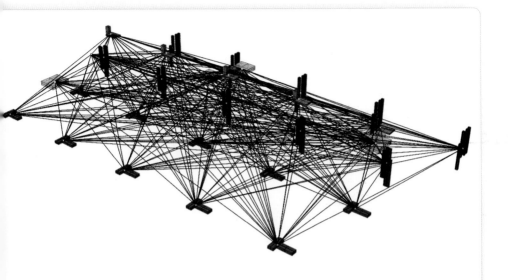

The main objective is for pathway networks to establish primary routes between major programmatic nodes. The establishment of connections between all major nodes then determines the location of major pathways, which are routes that still remain diagrams composed of lines. In order to become pathways, these lines must assume a specific volume appropriate for their traffic flow. Actual path size is dependent on many factors that will be explored in the following sections.

PROXIMITY

Proximity affects the likely probability that a person will use any given route at any given time (i.e. it is more likely for an individual to buy coffee at a coffee shop around the corner, rather than a coffee shop ten miles away). For the purposes of this discussion, we term this natural occurrence as likelihood,* represented as a percentage. In order to evaluate potential pathway usage, Nodes were assigned a programmatic title and number.

PROXIMITY DISTANCE TEMPLATE The following statistics, based on these percentages, determined near, medium, and far connections between nodes (highlighted with corresponding colors of blue, dark green, and light green respectively).

SHOPPING	University 1	University 2	University 3	University 4	University 5	Industry
mall 1	23.3	14	4.2	4.2	2.5	23.3
mall 2	23.3	14	4.2	4.2	2.5	23.3
mall 3	23.3	14	17.5	4.2	5	6.3
mall 4	4.2	14	4.2	4.2	5	23.3
mall 5	4.2	14	17.5	17.5	5	6.3
mall 6	4.2	5	17.5	4.2	5	6.3
mall 7	4.2	5	17.5	17.5	23.3	1.6
mall 8	4.2	5	4.2	17.5	5	6.3
mall 9	4.2	5	4.2	17.5	23.3	1.6
mall 10	5	5	4.2	4.2	23.3	1.6

SHOPPING	Office 7	Office 8	Office 9	Office 10	Stadium 1	Stadium 2
mall 1	3.6	6.3	1.6	2.5	35	23.3
mall 2	5	6.3	1.6	2.5	4.2	23.3
mall 3	3.6	6.3	4.2	5	35	23.3
mall 4	3.6	6.3	1.6	5	4.2	5
mall 5	3.6	11.6	4.2	5	4.2	5
mall 6	3.6	11.6	4.2	5	4.2	5
mall 7	35	11.6	4.2	23.3	4.2	5
mall 8	3.6	11.6	4.2	5	4.2	5
mall 9	35	11.6	70	23.3	2.5	2.5
mall 10	3.6	11.6	4.2	23.3	2.5	2.5

SHOPPING	Stadium 9	Stadium 10	Stadium 11	Stadium 12	Stadium 13	Stadium 14
mall 1	3.1	8.8	3.6	3.1	4.2	6.3
mall 2	3.1	8.8	3.6	3.1	4.2	6.3
mall 3	35	8.8	23.3	3.1	17.5	11.6
mall 4	3.1	8.8	3.6	3.1	4.2	11.6
mall 5	35	8.8	23.3	35	17.5	11.6
mall 6	3.1	8.8	3.6	3.1	17.5	11.6
mall 7	3.1	8.8	23.3	35	17.5	11.6
mall 8	3.1	8.8	3.6	3.1	4.2	11.6
mall 9	3.1	12.5	3.6	3.1	4.2	6.3
mall 10	3.1	12.5	3.6	3.1	4.2	6.3

Because a pathway must be sized to accommodate peak traffic flow, the likelihood of usage was determined for peak hours. While a positive correlation appeared between likelihood and path length, further study was required.

'Likelihood is represented as a percentage based on a node's proximity to other programs.

Office 1	Office 2	Office 3	Office 4	Office 5	Office 6
35	17.5	3.1	11.6	3.1	6.3
3.6	17.5	3.1	11.6	3.1	6.3
35	17.5	35	11.6	3.1	11.6
3.6	17.5	3.1	11.6	3.1	11.6
3.6	6.3	35	11.6	35	11.6
3.6	6.3	3.1	11.6	3.1	11.6
3.6	6.3	3.1	6.3	35	11.6
3.6	6.3	3.1	6.3	3.1	11.6
3.6	2.5	3.1	6.3	3.1	6.3
5	2.5	3.1	6.3	3.1	6.3

Stadium 3	Stadium 4	Stadium 5	Stadium 6	Stadium 7	Stadium 8
17.5	23.3	35	17.5	14	11.6
17.5	3.6	4.2	4.2	5	11.6
17.5	23.3	35	17.5	14	11.6
17.5	3.6	4.2	17.5	14	11.6
6.3	23.3	4.2	17.5	14	11.6
6.3	3.6	4.2	4.2	14	11.6
6.3	3.6	4.2	4.2	5	6.3
6.3	3.6	4.2	4.2	5	6.3
2.5	3.6	2.5	4.2	5	6.3
2.5	3.6	2.5	4.2	5	6.3

Stadium 15	Stadium 16	Stadium 17	Stadium 18	Stadium 19	Stadium 20
12.5	4.2	4.2	3.6	6.3	6.3
12.5	5	5	3.6	6.3	6.3
8.8	4.2	4.2	3.6	6.3	6.3
8.8	4.2	4.2	3.6	6.3	6.3
8.8	23.3	23.3	23.3	11.6	11.6
8.8	4.2	4.2	3.6	11.6	11.6
8.8	23.3	23.3	23.3	11.6	11.6
8.8	4.2	4.2	3.6	11.6	11.6
8.8	23.5	23.5	23.3	11.6	11.6
8.8	4.2	4.2	3.6	11.6	11.6

SHOPPING	Stadium 21	Stadium 22	Stadium 23	Stadium 24	Stadium 25	University 1
mall 1	1.6	2.5	2.5	2.5	1.6	17.5
mall 2	1.6	2.5	2.5	2.5	1.6	17.5
mall 3	5	5	6.3	6.3	4.2	17.5
mall 4	1.6	5	6.3	6.3	1.6	17.5
mall 5	5	5	6.3	6.3	4.2	6.3
mall 6	5	5	6.3	6.3	4.2	6.3
mall 7	35	23.3	17.5	17.5	4.2	6.3
mall 8	5	5	17.5	17.5	4.2	6.3
mall 9	35	23.3	17.5	17.5	70	2.5
mall 10	5	23.3	17.5	17.5	4.2	2.5

UNIVERSITIES	Stadium 1	Stadium 2	Stadium 3	Stadium 4	Stadium 5	Stadium 6
university 1	35	35	23.3	23.3	23.3	23.3
university 2	35	35	23.3	23.3	23.3	23.3
university 3	12.5	12.5	23.3	23.3	23.3	23.3
university 4	12.5	12.5	35	12.5	12.5	12.5
university 5	5	5	5	12.5	12.5	12.5

UNIVERSITIES	Stadium 11	Stadium 12	Stadium 13	Stadium 14	Stadium 15	Stadium 16
university 1	12.5	25	12.5	25	8.3	12.5
university 2	23.3	17.5	23.3	17.5	8.3	12.5
university 3	23.3	17.5	23.3	17.5	35	23.3
university 4	23.3	17.5	23.3	17.5	35	23.3
university 5	12.5	17.5	12.5	17.5	8.3	23.3

UNIVERSITIES	Stadium 21	Stadium 22	Stadium 23	Stadium 24	Stadium 25	Industry
university 1	5	5	5	5	5	35
university 2	12.5	12.5	12.5	8.3	12.5	35
university 3	12.5	12.5	12.5	8.3	12.5	12.5
university 4	35	35	35	8.3	35	12.5
university 5	35	35	35	70	35	5

UNIVERSITIES	University 1	University 2	University 3	University 4	University 5	Industry
stadium 1	7.8	5	2.8	2.8	1.7	7
stadium 2	7.8	5	2.8	2.8	1.7	7
stadium 3	7.8	5	4.4	2.8	1.7	7
stadium 4	7.8	5	4.4	2.8	2.5	7
stadium 5	7.8	5	4.4	2.8	2.5	7
stadium 6	7.8	5	4.4	2.8	2.5	7
stadium 7	7.8	5	4.4	4.4	2.5	7
stadium 8	7.8	5	2.8	2.8	2.5	7
stadium 9	7.8	5	4.4	4.4	2.5	7
stadium 10	2.3	5	4.4	2.8	2.5	7
stadium 11	2.3	5	4.4	4.4	2.5	2.8
stadium 12	2.3	5	4.4	4.4	5.8	2.8
stadium 13	2.3	5	4.4	4.4	2.5	2.8

University 2	University 3	University 4	University 5
11.6	8.7	12.5	6.3
11.6	8.7	12.5	6.3
11.6	8.7	8.7	6.3
11.6	8.7	8.7	6.3
11.6	8.7	8.7	11.6
11.6	8.7	8.7	11.6
6.3	8.7	8.7	11.6
6.3	8.7	8.7	11.6
6.3	12.5	8.7	11.6
6.3	12.5	8.7	11.6

Stadium 7	Stadium 8	Stadium 9	Stadium 10
17.5	35	17.5	8.3
17.5	35	17.5	35
17.5	8.3	17.5	35
17.5	8.3	17.5	8.3
25	8.3	25	8.3

Stadium 17	Stadium 18	Stadium 19	Stadium 20
12.5	12.5	12.5	8.3
12.5	12.5	12.5	8.3
23.3	23.3	23.3	8.3
23.3	23.3	23.3	35
23.3	23.3	23.3	35

UNIVERSITIES	University 1	University 2	University 3	University 4	University 5	Industry
stadium 14	2.3	5	4.4	4.4	5.8	2.8
stadium 15	2.3	2.3	4.4	4.4	2.5	2.8
stadium 16	2.3	2.3	14.4	4.4	5.8	2.8
stadium 17	2.3	2.3	4.4	4.4	5.8	2.8
stadium 18	2.3	2.3	4.4	4.4	5.8	0.8
stadium 19	2.3	2.3	4.4	4.4	5.8	2.8
stadium 20	2.3	2.3	2.8	4.4	5.8	2.8
stadium 21	1	2.3	2.8	4.4	5.8	0.8
stadium 22	1	2.3	2.8	4.4	5.8	0.8
stadium 23	1	2.3	2.8	4.4	5.8	0.8
stadium 24	1	2.3	2.8	2.8	5.8	0.8
stadium 25	1	2.3	2.8	4.4	5.8	0.8

OFFICE PARKS	Mall 1	Mall 2	Mall 3	Mall 4	Mall 5	Mall 6
Office 1	23.3	5	14	4.2	5	3.5
Office 2	23.3	35	14	23.3	5	3.5
Office 3	5	5	14	4.2	14	3.5
Office 4	23.3	35	14	23.3	14	23.3
Office 5	5	5	6.3	4.2	14	3.5
Office 6	5	5	14	23.3	14	23.3
Office 7	5	1.6	6.3	4.2	5	3.5
Office 8	5	5	6.3	4.2	14	23.3
Office 9	2.5	1.6	6.3	5	5	3.5
Office 10	2.5	1.6	6.3	4.2	5	3.5

OFFICE PARKS	Stadium 1	Stadium 2	Stadium 3	Stadium 4	Stadium 5	Stadium 6
Office 1	17.5	17.5	17.5	11.6	17.5	11.6
Office 2	17.5	17.5	17.5	11.6	17.5	11.6
Office 3	17.5	17.5	17.5	11.6	17.5	11.6
Office 4	17.5	17.5	17.5	11.6	17.5	11.6
Office 5	6.3	6.3	6.3	11.6	6.3	11.6
Office 6	6.3	6.3	6.3	11.6	6.3	11.6
Office 7	6.3	6.3	6.3	8.3	6.3	6.3
Office 8	6.3	6.3	6.3	8.3	6.3	6.3
Office 9	2.5	2.5	2.5	5	2.5	6.3
Office 10	2.5	2.5	2.5	8.3	2.5	6.3

OFFICE PARKS	Stadium 14	Stadium 15	Stadium 16	Stadium 17	Stadium 18	Stadium 19
Office 1	8.7	4.2	8.3	6.3	12.5	12.5
Office 2	8.7	4.2	8.3	6.3	12.5	12.5
Office 3	8.7	4.2	1	6.3	8.7	8.7
Office 4	8.7	17.5	8.3	6.3	8.7	8.7
Office 5	8.7	17.5	1	11.6	8.7	8.7
Office 6	8.7	17.5	1	11.6	8.7	8.7
Office 7	8.7	4.2	1	11.6	8.7	8.7
Office 8	8.7	17.5	1	11.6	8.7	8.7
Office 9	8.3	4.2	1	11.6	8.7	8.7
Office 10	8.3	4.2	1	11.6	8.7	8.7

STADIUMS	University 1	University 2	University 3	University 4	University 5	Industry
stadium 1	7.8	5	2.8	2.8	1.7	7
stadium 2	7.8	5	2.8	2.8	1.7	7
stadium 3	7.8	5	4.4	2.8	1.7	7
stadium 4	7.8	5	4.4	2.8	2.5	7
stadium 5	7.8	5	4.4	2.8	2.5	7
stadium 6	7.8	5	4.4	2.8	2.5	7
stadium 7	7.8	5	4.4	4.4	2.5	7
stadium 8	7.8	5	2.8	2.8	2.5	7
stadium 9	7.8	5	4.4	4.4	2.5	7
stadium 10	2.3	5	4.4	2.8	2.5	7
stadium 11	2.3	5	4.4	4.4	2.5	2.8
stadium 12	2.3	5	4.4	4.4	5.8	2.8
stadium 13	2.3	5	4.4	4.4	2.5	2.8
stadium 14	2.3	5	4.4	4.4	5.8	2.8

Mall 7	Mall 8	Mall 9	Mall 10
5	3.1	5	1.6
5	3.1	5	1.6
5	3.1	5	5
5	3.1	5	5
14	3.1	5	5
14	35	5	5
14	3.1	17.5	5
14	35	17.5	35
5	3.1	17.5	1.6
14	3.1	17.5	35

Stadium 7	Stadium 8	Stadium 9	Stadium 10	Stadium 11	Stadium 12	Stadium 13
11.6	17.5	11.6	5	1	6.3	8.7
11.6	17.5	11.6	17.5	8.3	6.3	8.7
11.6	6.3	11.6	17.5	1	11.6	8.7
11.6	17.5	11.6	17.5	1	11.6	8.7
11.6	6.3	11.6	5	1	11.6	8.7
11.6	17.5	11.6	17.5	1	11.6	8.7
14	6.3	6.3	5	1	11.6	8.7
14	6.3	6.3	5	1	11.6	8.7
5	2.5	6.3	5	8.3	6.3	8.3
8.3	2.5	6.3	5	8.3	6.3	8.3

Stadium 20	Stadium 21	Stadium 22	Stadium 23	Stadium 24	Stadium 25
4.2	6.3	2.5	8.3	8.3	2.5
4.2	5	2.5	5	5	2.5
4.2	6.3	6.3	8.3	8.3	5
4.2	6.3	6.3	8.3	8.3	5
4.2	14	6.3	11.6	11.6	5
17.5	6.3	6.3	11.6	11.6	5
17.5	14	17.5	11.6	11.6	5
17.5	14	17.5	11.6	11.6	23.3
4.2	14	17.5	11.6	11.6	23.3
17.5	14	17.5	11.6	11.6	23.3

STADIUMS	University 1	University 2	University 3	University 4	University 5	Industry
stadium 15	2.3	2.3	4.4	4.4	2.5	2.8
stadium 16	2.3	2.3	4.4	4.4	5.8	2.8
stadium 17	2.3	2.3	4.4	4.4	5.8	2.8
stadium 18	2.3	2.3	4.4	4.4	5.8	0.8
stadium 19	2.3	2.3	4.4	4.4	5.8	2.8
stadium 20	2.3	2.3	2.8	4.4	5.8	2.8
stadium 21	1	2.3	2.8	4.4	5.8	0.8
stadium 22	1	2.3	2.8	4.4	5.8	0.8
stadium 23	1	2.3	2.8	4.4	5.8	0.8
stadium 24	1	2.3	2.8	2.8	5.8	0.8
stadium 25	1	2.3	2.8	4.4	5.8	0.8

STADIUMS	Mall 1	Mall 2	Mall 3	Mall 4	Mall 5	Mall 6
stadium 1	7.8	1.8	5	1.6	3.1	1.6
stadium 2	7.8	17.5	5	1.6	3.1	1.6
stadium 3	7.8	17.5	5	10	3.1	1.6
stadium 4	7.8	1.8	5	1.6	4.4	1.6
stadium 5	7.8	1.8	5	1.6	3.1	1.6
stadium 6	7.8	1.8	5	10	4.4	1.6
stadium 7	7.8	1.8	5	10	4.4	8.8
stadium 8	7.8	17.5	5	10	4.4	8.8
stadium 9	2.3	1.8	5	1.6	4.4	1.6
stadium 10	7.8	17.5	5	10	4.4	8.8
stadium 11	2.3	1.8	5	1.6	4.4	1.6
stadium 12	2.3	1.8	2.5	1.6	4.4	1.6
stadium 13	2.3	1.8	5	1.6	4.4	8.8
stadium 14	2.3	1.8	5	10	4.4	8.8
stadium 15	2.3	1.8	5	10	4.4	8.8
stadium 16	2.3	0.7	2.5	1.6	4.4	1.6
stadium 17	2.3	0.7	2.5	1.6	4.4	1.6
stadium 18	2.3	1.8	2.5	1.6	4.4	1.6
stadium 19	2.3	1.8	2.5	1.6	4.4	8.8
stadium 20	2.3	1.8	2.5	1.6	4.4	8.8
stadium 21	1	0.7	5	2.5	5	5
stadium 22	1	0.7	2.5	1.6	3.1	1.6
stadium 23	1	0.7	2.5	1.6	3.1	1.6
stadium 24	1	0.7	2.5	1.6	3.1	1.6
stadium 25	1	0.7	2.5	2.5	3.1	1.6

STADIUMS	Office 1	Office 2	Office 3	Office 4	Office 5	Office 6
stadium 1	5.8	5.8	4.4	4.1	2.8	3.6
stadium 2	5.8	5.8	4.4	4.1	2.8	3.6
stadium 3	5.8	5.8	4.4	4.1	2.8	3.6
stadium 4	5.8	5.8	4.4	4.1	4.4	3.9
stadium 5	5.8	5.8	4.4	4.1	2.8	3.6
stadium 6	5.8	5.8	4.4	4.1	4.4	3.9
stadium 7	5.8	5.8	4.4	4.1	4.4	3.9
stadium 8	5.8	5.8	2.8	4.1	2.8	3.9
stadium 9	5.8	5.8	4.4	4.1	4.4	3.9
stadium 10	2.3	5.8	4.4	4.1	2.8	3.9
stadium 11	5.8	3.1	4.4	4.1	4.4	3.9
stadium 12	2.3	3.1	4.4	4.1	4.4	3.9
stadium 13	5.8	5.8	4.4	4.1	4.4	3.9
stadium 14	5.8	5.8	4.4	4.1	4.4	3.9
stadium 15	2.3	3.1	2.8	4.1	4.4	3.9
stadium 16	2.3	3.1	4.4	3.1	4.4	3.9
stadium 17	2.3	3.1	2.8	3.1	4.4	3.9
stadium 18	2.3	3.1	4.4	4.1	4.4	3.9
stadium 19	2.3	3.1	4.4	4.1	4.4	3.9
stadium 20	2.3	3.1	2.8	3.1	2.8	3.9
stadium 21	2.3	1	2.8	3.1	4.4	3.6
stadium 22	2.5	1	2.8	3.1	2.8	3.6
stadium 23	2.3	1	2.8	3.1	4.4	3.9
stadium 24	2.3	1	2.8	3.1	4.4	3.9
stadium 25	2.5	1	2.8	3.1	2.8	3.6

Mall 7	Mall 8	Mall 9	Mall 10
2.5	1.5	1.3	1
2.5	1.5	1.3	1
2.5	1.5	1.3	1
2.5	1.5	2.5	1.8
2.5	1.5	1.3	1
2.5	1.5	2.5	1.8
2.5	1.5	2.5	1.8
2.5	1.5	2.5	1.8
2.5	1.5	2.5	1.8
4.7	10	2.5	1.8
4.7	1.5	2.5	1.8
4.7	1.5	2.5	1.8
4.7	1.5	2.5	1.8
4.7	10	2.5	1.8
4.7	10	6.4	11.7
4.7	1.5	6.4	1.8
4.7	1.5	6.4	1.8
4.7	10	6.4	11.7
4.7	10	6.4	11.7
4.7	5	6.4	1
4.7	1.5	6.4	11.7
4.7	10	6.4	11.7
4.7	10	6.4	11.7
2.5	1.5	6.4	1.8

Office 7	Office 8	Office 9	Office 10
2.1	2.5	0.6	1
2.1	2.5	0.6	1
2.1	2.5	0.6	1
2.1	2.5	0.6	2.5
2.1	2.5	0.6	1
2.1	2.5	3.1	2.5
2.1	2.5	0.6	2.5
2.1	2.5	0.6	1
2.1	2.5	3.1	2.5
2.1	2.5	0.6	2.5
5.4	4.7	3.1	2.5
5.4	4.7	3.1	2.5
5.4	4.7	3.1	2.5
5.4	4.7	3.1	2.5
2.1	4.7	3.1	2.5
5.4	4.7	7.8	7
5.4	4.7	7.8	7
5.4	4.7	7.8	7
5.4	4.7	7.8	7
5.4	4.7	3.1	7
5.4	4.7	7.8	7
5.4	4.7	7.8	7
5.4	4.7	7.8	7
2.1	4.7	7.8	7

PROXIMITY / Visualization of Parameters

These diagrams illustrate varying paths: paths that are near connections, medium connections, and far connections between nodes. They are a visualization of the proximity parameter.

Complete Network

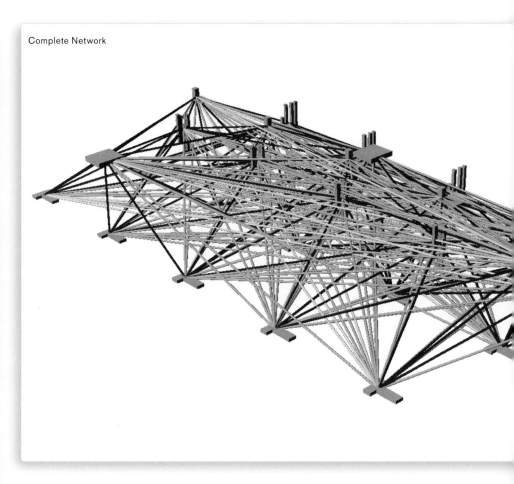

Partial Network

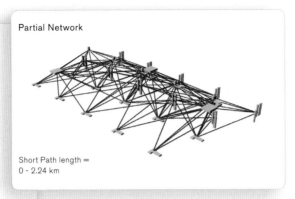

Short Path length =
0 - 2.24 km

Partial Network

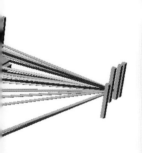
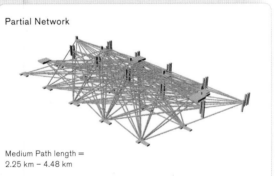

Medium Path length =
2.25 km – 4.48 km

Partial Network

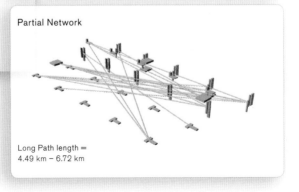

Long Path length =
4.49 km – 6.72 km

PROXIMITY / Capacity

Evaluation of likelihood provided an estimation of how many cars might actually travel along each pathway at peak hours. Which pathways are low, medium, or high capacity? Certain programmatic requirements exert their influence on the final determination of each pathway's capacity. However, spatial requirements of the skycar remain undefined.

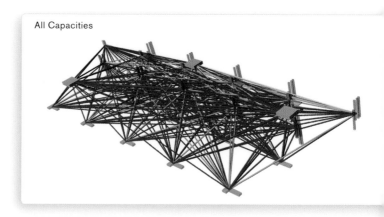

All Capacities

PROXIMITY / G-Force

G-Force: G-force is used primarily in aerospace fields, where it represents a magnitude for the loads on aircraft and spacecraft (and their pilots or passengers). For instance, most civilian aircrafts are capable of being stressed to 4.33 g (42.5 m/s; 139 ft/s), which is considered a safe value. G-force is also used in automotive engineering, primarily in relation to cornering forces and collision analysis.

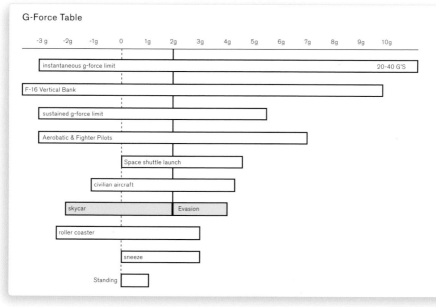

G-Force Table

-3 g	-2g	-1g	0	1g	2g	3g	4g	5g	6g	7g	8g	9g	10g

instantaneous g-force limit .... 20-40 G'S

F-16 Vertical Bank

sustained g-force limit

Aerobatic & Fighter Pilots

Space shuttle launch

civilian aircraft

skycar / Evasion

roller coaster

sneeze

Standing

High Capacity

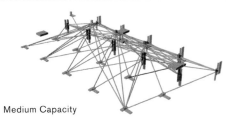

Medium Capacity

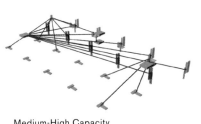

Medium-High Capacity

Low Capacity

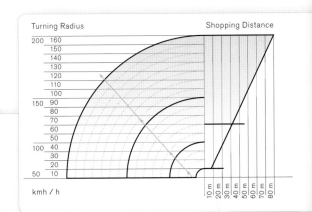

Turning Radius

Shopping Distance

200 160
150
140
130
120
110
100
150 90
80
70
60
50
100 40
30
20
50 10

kmh / h

10 m 20 m 30 m 40 m 50 m 60 m 70 m 80 m

G-forces for acceleration, decceleration, and turning are considered.

x = # of g - forces
m = mass
$v0$ = initial velocity
vt = final velocity
r = radius of turn
g = 9.8 m/s2
t = time
d = displacement

$$d = \frac{v0^2 - vt^2}{2 \cdot x \cdot g} \qquad r = \frac{v^2}{x \cdot g}$$

REACTION TIME COMPONENTS

Mental Processing Time - the time it takes for the driver to perceive that a signal has occurred and to decide upon a response.

Movement Time - Once a response is selected, the driver must perform the required muscle movements: for example, the time taken to apply the brakes of a car.

Device Response Time - Mechanical devices take time to activate, even after the driver has acted: for example, a driver stepping on the brake pedal does not stop the car immediately. Instead, the stopping is a function of physical forces, gravity and friction.

The turning radius of a skycar involves speed and tolerable g-force magnitude. If the passengers are allowed to experience a maximum of 4g relative to the speed that they are traveling, we can determine what the minimum turning radius for any speed would be.

PROXIMITY / Buffer Zone

The buffer zone influences how multiple skycars are allowed to aggregate when flying in various traffic situations (assuming manual mode). Varying numbers of skycars result in different sizes and shapes of space. Additionally, the dimension required for the paths varies depending upon overlapping versus tangent buffer zones; the latter assumes a higher degree of safety within the cross section. The tangent buffer zone is immense in size, which thereby limits the volume of cars possible in the cross section.

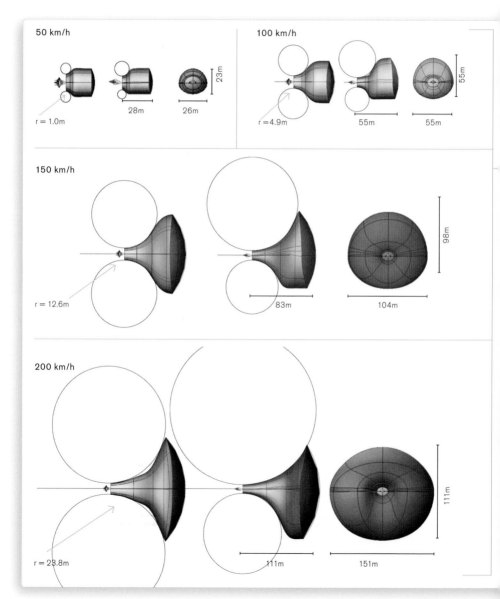

50 km/h

23m

28m   26m

r = 1.0m

100 km/h

55m

55m   55m

r = 4.9m

150 km/h

98m

83m   104m

r = 12.6m

200 km/h

111m

111m   151m

r = 23.8m

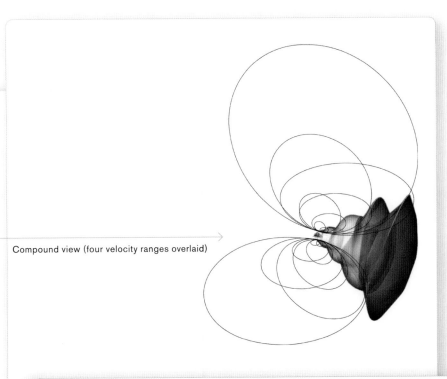

Compound view (four velocity ranges overlaid)

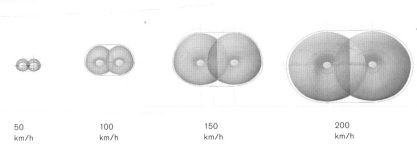

| 50 km/h | 100 km/h | 150 km/h | 200 km/h |

/ Buffer Zone // Cross Section
When the previous factors are combined, the resultant safety buffer zone has a very specific shape dependent upon speed. (All diagrams show buffer zones in plan, side, and frontal views). All views are drawn at the same relative scale.

The relationship between speed, buffer zone, and capacity was analyzed to inform pathway dimensions. A significant factor in the determination of dimension involved the consideration of overlapping or tangent buffer zones, (assuming manual, not computer-automated navigation). Clearly, a conservative dimension would consider the buffer zones as tangent to one another; yet this configuration results in dimensions at times 100% larger than overlapped buffer zones. Accordingly, overlapped configurations are more spatially efficient, while tangential configurations are safer. We opted to further study a combination of these configurations, depending on one or two-way traffic requirements.

NUMBER OF VEHICLES	VOLUME	DIAGRAM (OVERLAPPING / TANGENT)
2	170m x 97m vs. 210m x 97m	
3	165m x152m vs. 210m x 180m	
4	165m x 160m vs. 210m x 195m	
5	165m x 193m vs. 268m x 195m	
6	263m x 160m vs. 393m x 195m	
7	225m x 205m vs. 286m x 295m	

NUMBER OF VEHICLES	VOLUME	DIAGRAM (OVERLAPPING / TANGENT)	
8	287m x 220m vs. 415m x 295m		
9	287m x 205m vs. 315m x 295m		
10	287m x 205m vs. 415m x 270m		
11	287m x 256m vs. 415m x 368m		
12	287m x 285m vs. 415m x 350m		

PROXIMITY / Passing

Currently, typical highways for automobiles do not assume an overly-conservative safety zone for vehicles, with the understanding that other methods of safety such as mirrors, spatial awareness of the driver, safety lights and horns can assist in the avoidance of accidents. Skycars are equipped with a similar range of safety features, as well as new features such as magnetic bumpers, shock absorbing frames, and automated avoidance precautions.

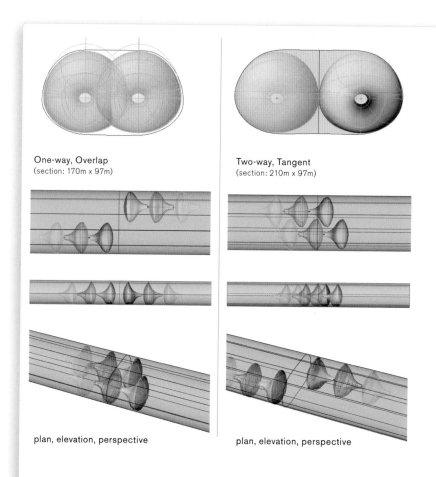

One-way, Overlap
(section: 170m x 97m)

Two-way, Tangent
(section: 210m x 97m)

plan, elevation, perspective

plan, elevation, perspective

PATHWAY DIMENSIONS (scenarios) The buffer zone and clustering configurations determine the amount of space required for passing in one-way and two-way traffic conditions. In one-way travel, the use of skycar safety features allows for greater spatial efficiency within the path. Hence, the buffer zones in the one-way cross section of the future pathway will operate with overlapping fields (as it does today); In two-way travel, skycars are moving in opposing directions, requiring buffer zones to remain tangent to one another. The fields may not overlap in order to avoid head-on collisions.

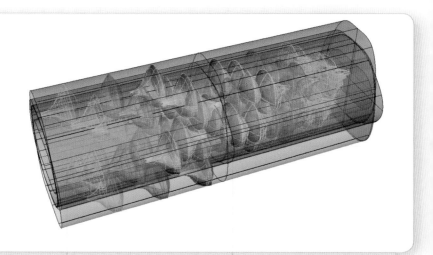

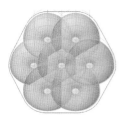

One-way , 7 car
(section: 225m x 205m)

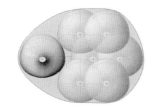

Two-way II, 7 car
(section: 210m x 97m)

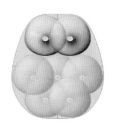

Two-way I, 7 car
(section: 170m x 97m)

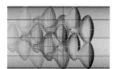

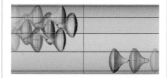

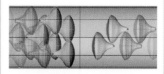

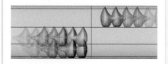

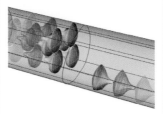

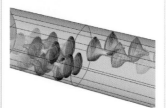

plan, elevation, perspective

plan, elevation, perspective

plan, elevation, perspective

PATHWAY CONFIGURATION

Considering the capacity requirements from earlier studies and the dimensional results of the cross section studies (revealing possible pathway dimensions related to skycar capacity), four levels of pathway capacity and configuration were determined.

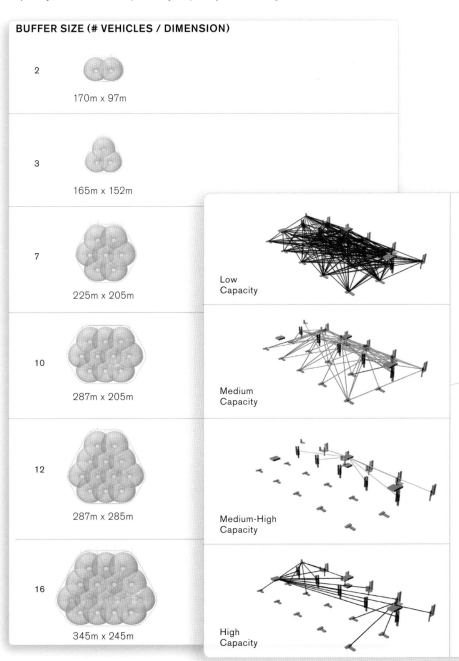

BUFFER SIZE (# VEHICLES / DIMENSION)

2		170m x 97m
3		165m x 152m
7		225m x 205m
10		287m x 205m
12		287m x 285m
16		345m x 245m

Low Capacity

Medium Capacity

Medium-High Capacity

High Capacity

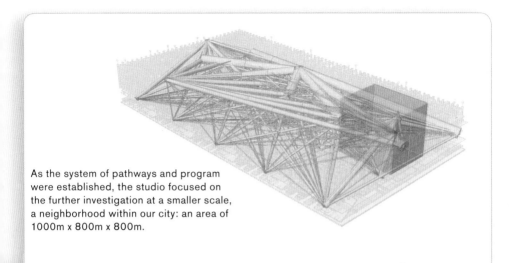

As the system of pathways and program were established, the studio focused on the further investigation at a smaller scale, a neighborhood within our city: an area of 1000m x 800m x 800m.

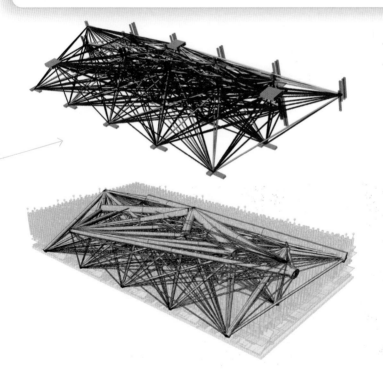

Each colored line describes a tube that can accommodate hypothetical peak traffic flow and buffer zones. The exercise produced a conceptual diagram of pathways in the city. This set of conceptual tubes represents the sized pathway system in our city, a pathway system that will form the main circulation routes in the city.

ORIGIN OF NODES AND THEIR FORMATION / Bundling Pathways

A closer look at the complex network of pathways yielded the possibility that some paths were redundant. Could redundant pathways fuse or bundle in order to create a more efficient network of fewer pathways that would still accommodate the same amount of traffic? The string model images represent the pathway network before and after examination of redundancy and efficiency. The results of bundling reduced the overall complexity of the pathway system, releasing more space to be occupied by program or non-pathway open space.

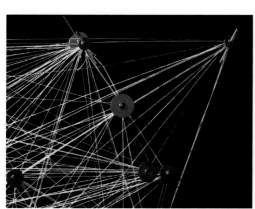

Before Bundling

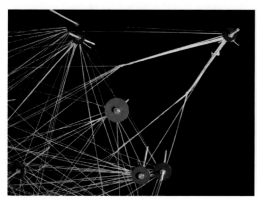

After Bundling

From Bundling to Nodes

1. Begin with bundled pathway.

2. Pathways sized to proper capacities and buffer sizes.

3. Addition of deceleration and exiting zone.

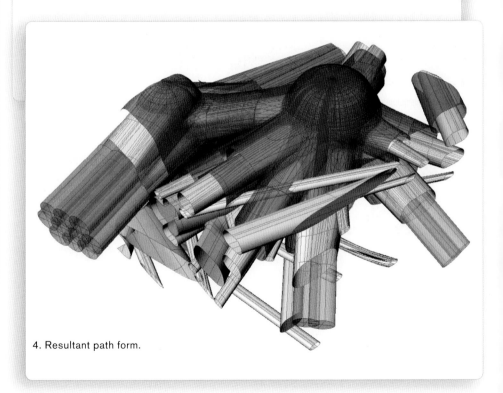

4. Resultant path form.

ORIGIN OF NODES AND THEIR FORMATION / Node Development

An intersection near the university was further explored in order to study several different components: The crossing of two main pathways/ Exiting from a large pathway to a smaller pathway/ The merging zone/ Tendril pathways/ Polyp spaces.

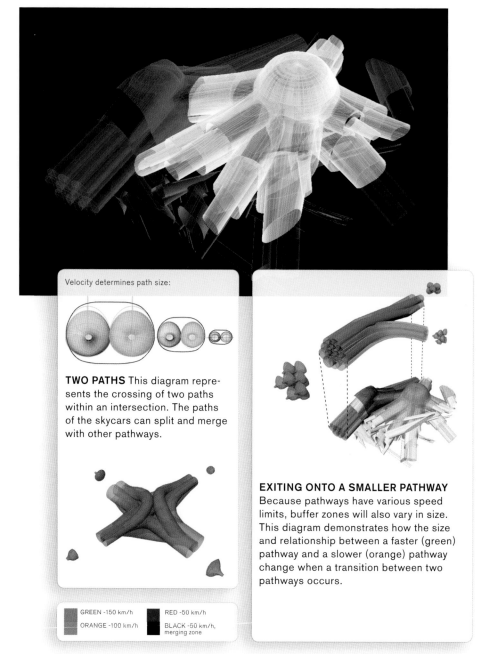

Velocity determines path size:

TWO PATHS This diagram represents the crossing of two paths within an intersection. The paths of the skycars can split and merge with other pathways.

EXITING ONTO A SMALLER PATHWAY
Because pathways have various speed limits, buffer zones will also vary in size. This diagram demonstrates how the size and relationship between a faster (green) pathway and a slower (orange) pathway change when a transition between two pathways occurs.

GREEN -150 km/h

ORANGE -100 km/h

RED -50 km/h

BLACK -50 km/h, merging zone

MERGING AND WEAVING Merging zone of space in addition to the safety buffer creates another layer of space around the skycars, ultimately increasing the diameter of the pathways.

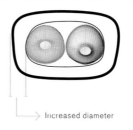

→ Increased diameter

Merging Zone

Extra Space

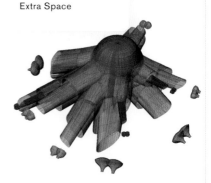

The driver joins the movement onto a primary skypath via a merging zone (much akin to the exit/entry ramps of today's typical highways), indicated in red. However, in the case of skycars, the merge zone surrounds the path, allowing merging to occur above, below, and to the side. This merging zone forms an additional, 3-D "sheath" to accommodate entry and exit.

Here the offset of the merging zone is represented by a grey shell that delineates the limit of the extra zone of space around the pathways.

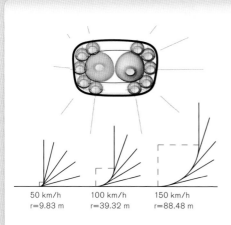

50 km/h	100 km/h	150 km/h
r=9.83 m	r=39.32 m	r=88.48 m

Tendrils

From the inside of the pathways, exits and entrances to the tendril pathways merge with larger routes.

EXITS AND ENTRIES Skycars are able to veer off into this merging zone and slow down, decreasing the necessary safety buffer size. The skycars are then able to exit onto smaller types of pathways, or "tendrils."

ORIGIN OF POLYPS AND THEIR FORMATION

TRANSITIONS Tendril paths are used to make sharp turns between adjacent larger pathways. The tendrils are only used in this manner when the turning angle is so sharp that the skycars must slow down in order to exit safely.

EXITS Tendrils are also used as exits off of the pathway system. Since these tendrils are exits to specific or groups of specific destinations, they are also small pathways that accommodate the relatively minor amount of traffic at each exit.

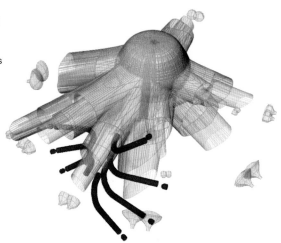

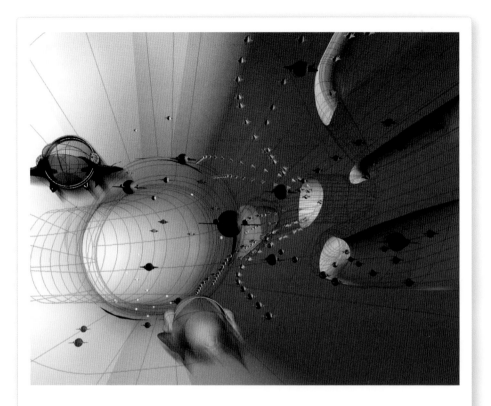

POLYPS The endpoints of many tendril pathways are "polyps." Polyps are voids of space that hold the entrances to a collection of destinations. They are comparable to neighborhoods or blocks in the city. One's address might be linked to a specific polyp in addition to specific 3-D coordinates.

An exterior abstraction of skypaths perforated by a series of "landing zones" that may serve as parking areas and/or entries to various program.

Baseball Arena,
Rendered view

POLYP DEVELOPMENT These images explored the potential of "pushing through" the program offset directly from the path. The 'polyp' concept describes specific program pieces such as a theater or a parking strategy. The polyp offers greater flexibility within the pathway network. The polyps, viewed from within the garden, vary in size and program use. Each polyp might assume various program types and sizes but also develop specific characteristics individual to that polyp. The polyp might produce neighborhood identity and, perhaps, a means of way-finding within the city.

POTENTIAL POLYP DENSITY
*The polyps could be mass
parking areas or open voids
for program.

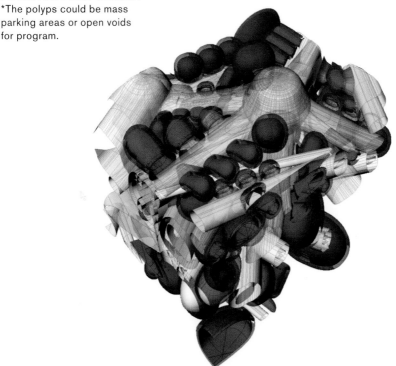

The resulting pathway and polyp diagram suggests an organism not unlike that of the
human body. This organism offers a legible, yet supple circulation system consisting
of primary, secondary, and tertiary vessels, the metrics of which grow naturally from
the physics of skycar movement. This circulation system is inherently flexible –capable
of absorbing further alteration and complexity. The resultant interstitial spaces are
occupied by polyps, mutable void spaces that are supported by the circulation system
and formed by their imagined purpose.

**The polyps have the
potential to play a
specialized role in the
city. Upon this armature,
the studio investigated
urban form, considering
the relationship between
speed, action, technology,
and destination.**

PARKING

Serving as an interface between pathway and program, parking strategies and concepts were developed based on skycar requirements and parking type (i.e. landing, linking, magnetizing), as well as innovative and specific types of parking that take advantage of the 3-dimensional character of skycars. Examples vary related to the time required to remain in a parking spot, landing methods, and new concepts of program that utilize the ability to fly.

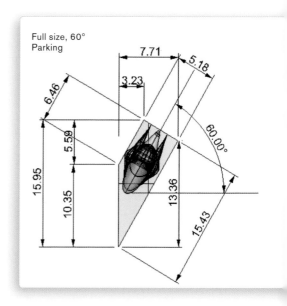

Full size, 60°
Parking

PARKING STRUCTURE DEVELOPMENT

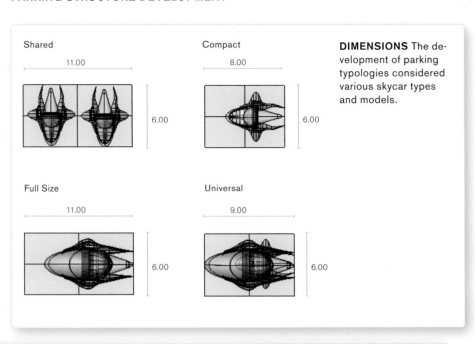

Shared

11.00

6.00

Compact

8.00

6.00

DIMENSIONS The development of parking typologies considered various skycar types and models.

Full Size

11.00

6.00

Universal

9.00

6.00

Full size, 40°
Parking

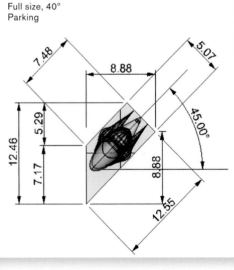

7.48
8.88
5.07
45.00°
12.46
5.29
7.17
8.88
12.55

PARKING 60° AND 40° Every dimension of the skycar factored into the overall parking configuration. (In this case, parking spots configured for 60° and 45°.)

PARKING STRUCTURE DEVELOPMENT

60° Parking

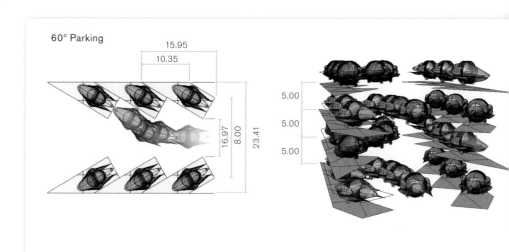

40° Parking

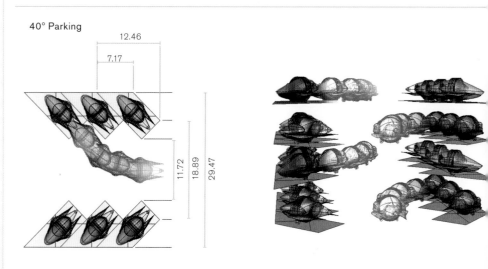

Side-by-Side Parking

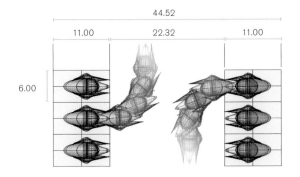

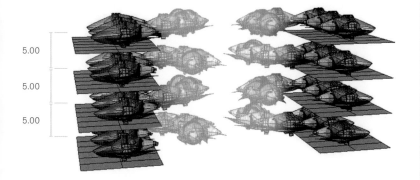

Elevation and section perspective

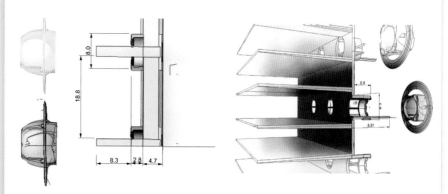

PRONG PARKING This strategic system is the basis for a number of potential parking strategies. It is comprised of a prong attached to a program element or pathway edge. The skycars with prongs can slide onto this prong for stable support over extended periods of time. An automated guidance system ensures proper alignment.

Plan and axonometric

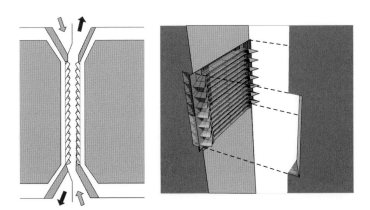

SKIP-STOP PARK This parking scheme allows skycars to land in a traditional angle format. The parking is situated within program and offers a skip-stop entrance and exit strategy. The levels of parking stack vertically as required by the related program.

Pentagonal format   Trianglular format   Rectangular format (plan view)

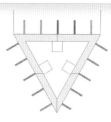
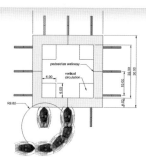

Rectangular format (axonometric view)

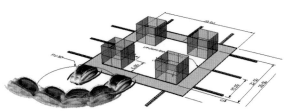

HANGING RACK This parking scheme is comprised of a rack hanging below program pieces. The racks utilize the prong landing system which connects to walkways and elevators. The parking scheme optimizes the spatial volume existing below program elements.

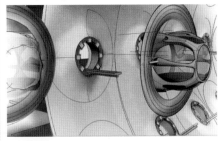

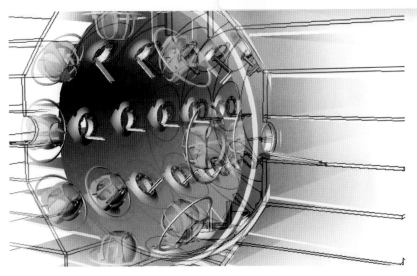

Cross-section views, long and transverse

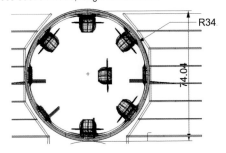

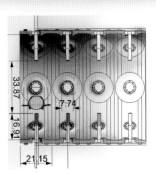

ROLODEX This parking scheme combines the prong landing system with magnetic linking options. Each ring in the drum revolves like a "rolodex" to offer more parking positions. The drum is activated via a call button, similar to an automated valet.

PARKING TYPOLOGIES / Honeycomb and Scallop

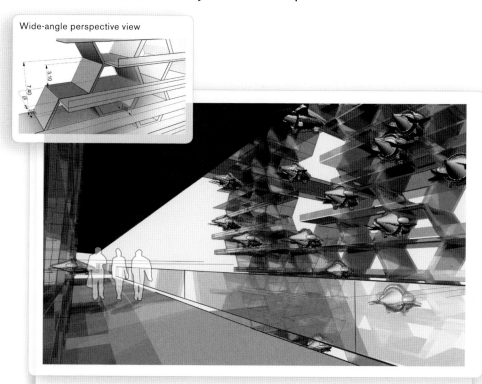

Wide-angle perspective view

Measured perspective view   Elevation

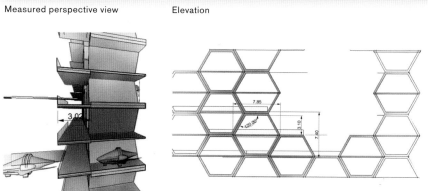

HONEYCOMB This strategy provides spaces for vehicles to land and sit. The one-sided nature of this scheme allows vehicles to enter from one side and easily fly out the other, over pedestrian walkways. This type of parking is situated within pathway spaces and assists in defining the fly zone.

Measured plan view

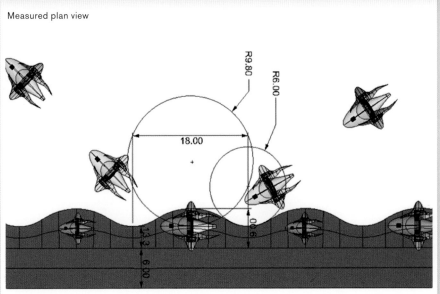

SCALLOP This parking strategy provides the equivalent of "street parking" to Skycar City. Positioned along the edges of pathways, these landing pads are shaped by the movement of vehicles and form a scalloped edge.

Wide-angle perspective view

Cross section perspective view

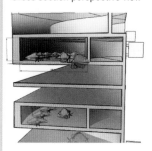

Interior perspective

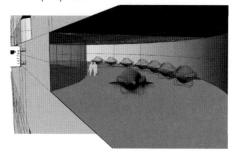

Measured plan

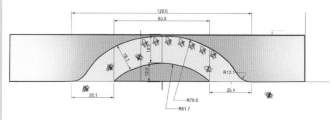

PASSAGE This parking scheme perforates the wall of the pathways to offer passages into the program. These passages contain short-term angle parking for vehicles to land. The double sided, one-way movement allows for efficient entry and exit.

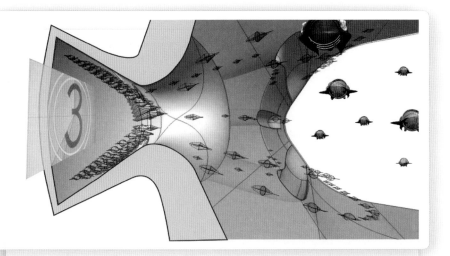

Measured plan and perspective view

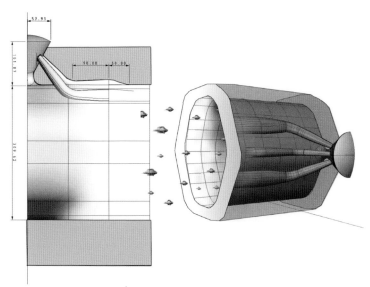

THEATER This parking concept is more specific to mass gatherings such as "fly-in" movies and other forms of entertainment. As a programmed polyp, the cars in this scheme hover in position or are attached via a prong or magnetic parking system. Funnels along the path provide merging zones and slower space as well as other entrances to the polyp volume.

Wide-angle perspective view

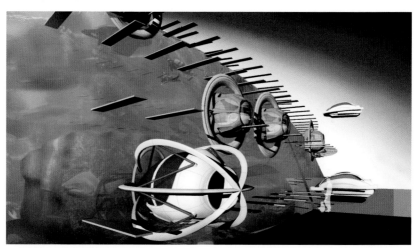

Perspective diagram

Measured plan and elevation

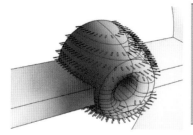

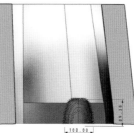

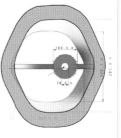

SKYQUARIUM This parking concept uses the prong parking system as an alternative way to imagine the relationship between parking and program; in this example, an aquarium was developed. This program element, or icon of a program element, dangles in the middle of a pathway. Skycars can latch onto the exterior of the tank or fly through a central void.

Wide-angle perspective view

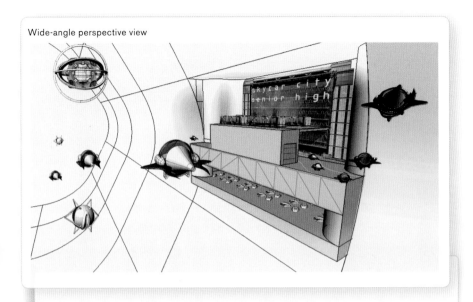

Program distribution diagram

Section perspective

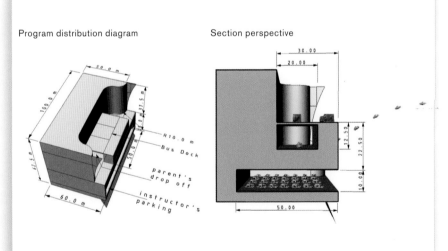

MULTI-MODAL Given the varying parking strategies, the multi-modal parking antici-
pates the integration of four parking modes in one building: individual pick-up/drop-
off, mass transit pick-up/drop off, short-term and long term parking. In this example,
mass transit is positioned on a "shelf" above a porte cochere; however, the sectional
position of each mode may be stacked in a variety of positions and configurations.

Football spectacle

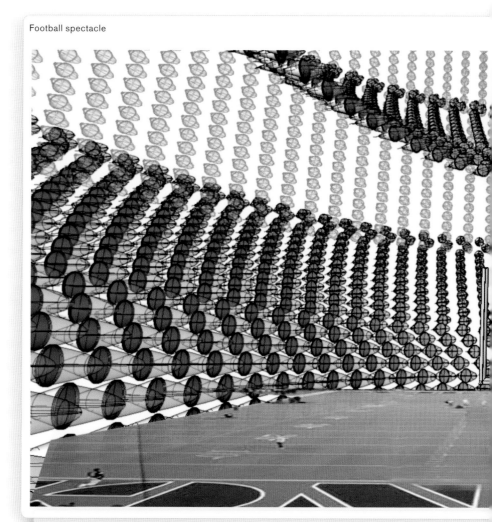

Axonometric, exterior perspective, and interior perspective

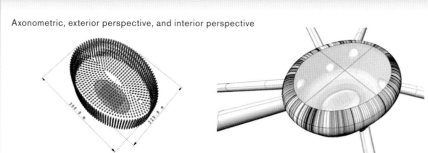

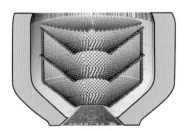

STADIUM Stadium parking re-conceptualizes mass gatherings, such as stadium related events in Skycar City. This concept takes advantage of the 3-D potential of skycars, providing optimal viewing position of the game; the parking lot serves as bleachers that become the stadium volume and define its edges.

CITY TYPOLOGIES

The following section offers hypothetical cities with more detailed explorations of the relationship between pathways, program, and urban form. In all the examples, the requirements of the pathways (developed in the earlier chapters) form the starting point for the generation of relationships between destinations within the city. Also, the program accommodates 5,000,000 inhabitants and selected destinations were evenly dispersed in a "centralized" fashion. The studies focused on a discrete section of the city, a neighborhood within the city, in order to more closely examine the interaction of skycar, its mode of movement, and its specific impact on urban form.

NEIGHBORHOOD LOCATION

The basic formal configuration of the city consists of a grid of programmatic volumes, connected by a system of pathways designed for maximum efficiency in circulation. This operation resulted in numerous moments in which program and pathways overlapped, crisscrossed, and conflicted, suggesting further areas of study and innovation.

	CITY	NEIGHBORHOOD
People	171,009	5,000,000
Skycars (2 per household)	148,703	4,347,826
Built Program Volume (km^3)	146.53	4,284.20
Size (m)	800x800x800	3200x5850x800
Total Area (sq. m)	640,000	18,720,000
Total Volume (km^3)	512.00	14,970.00
Program as % total volume	28.6%	28.6%
% Total program	100.00%	100.00%
Neighborhood path volume (km^3)	91.11	91.11
People per sq. km	267,201	267,201
Cubic m of program per skycar	985	985

In order to study the city in greater detail, the studio examined the potential of a neighborhood –a microcosm of the larger entity. These statistics represent base conditions (reflecting initial assumptions) for a city and its neighborhood subset. These statistics provide a standard against which the hypothetical cities can be measured and analyzed.

The hypothetical cities, neighborhoods of 800m wide x 800m deep x 800m tall, propose varying options for the relationship between pathway and program, testing for maximum advantages of the skycar. The attempt yielded four cities that combine the programmatic arrangement of the city with a pathway configuration: The Tower City, The Swiss Cheese City, The Coral City, and The Garden City. The parameters for these cities are presented in the following section.

As is represented in this image, the program clusters together into groups that form smaller blocks within a neighborhood. Paths are left unobstructed and horizontal masses can become pedestrian connections between the towers.

TYPE 1: **TOWER CITY**

The Tower City assumes the extrusion of highrises, evenly spaced for diagrammatic purposes. While limited in formal possibilities due to its over-reliance on rectilinear towers, this scheme usefully establishes the primary positions of program components. The scheme is not a radical departure from contemporary urban form, suggesting a subtler impact of the skycar on urban form.

Reshuffling the programmatic masses, the Tower City establishes a functional relationship between program and path. The original program distribution was re-ordered to maximize its relationship to the pathway network; where network is the primary organizing factor of the city and program subservient. This operation produced program clusters that occupied interstitial spaces between the pathways. The pathway network clearly specified where program could and could not be located as this arrange- ment simply moved program adjacent to and out of the way of the pathways.

Clustered programmatic elements formed smaller blocks within neighborhoods. Unobstructed paths and horizontal program masses created opportunities for the insertion of emergent landscapes and pedestrian connections bet- ween the towers. A cross section though the Tower City revealed this type's limitations: the dominance of a plane- metrically organized system precluded the potential use of space/real estate above and below the pathways. This unrealized potential suggested a simple "bending" of the towers to utilize the void space; however, such studies ge- nerally required further investigation into the 3-D character of urban form.

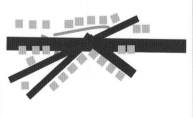

People	171,009
Skycars (2 per household)	148,703
Built Program Volume (km³)	146.53
Size (m)	800m3
Total Area (sq. m)	640,000
Total Volume (km³)	512.00
Program as % total volume	28.6%
% Total program	100.00%
Neighborhood path volume (km³)	91.11
People per sq. km	267,201
Cubic m of program per skycar	985
Density Rating	3rd

TOWER CITY /Mechanics

The towers gather around the path forming an edge. Courtyards develop on the other sides of the towers, an idea that will be revisited in another scheme.

Towers as edge

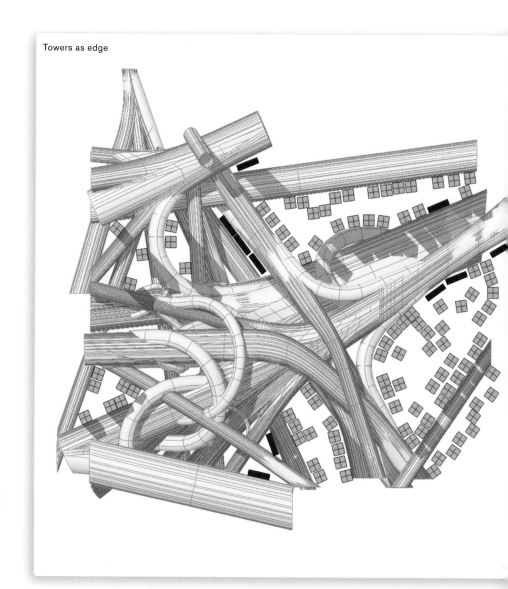

Courtyard Spaces (green)

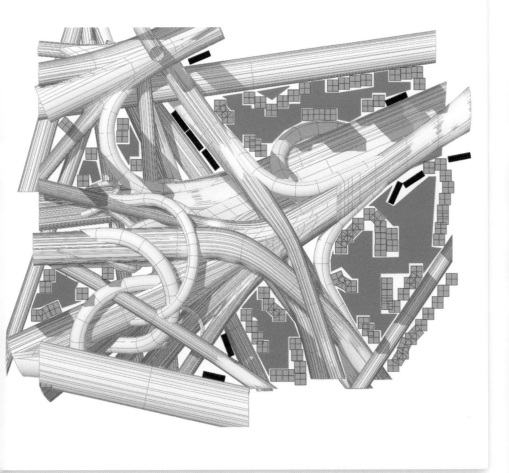

TOWER CITY /Programmatic Elements

As the pathway dimensions occupy a large percentage of the available area of the neighborhood, program elements are positioned within the interstitial space between the paths. The program elements are organized and clustered dependent upon available space and necessary access to path type (i.e. large, high-speed paths connect areas of shopping, while smaller pathways connect networks of housing or schools).

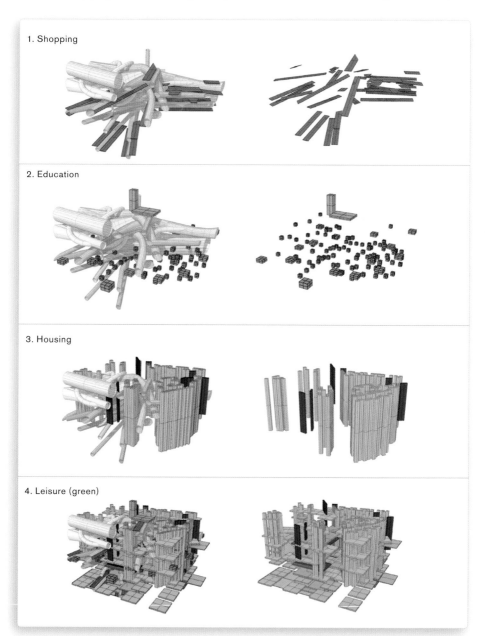

1. Shopping

2. Education

3. Housing

4. Leisure (green)

ENTERTAINMENT: The residual space between towers and paths creates an entertainment zone, a "fly-in" theater.

LEISURE: Newly found "ground" planes, uplifted terraces, and rooftops offer redefinition of open space and parkland.

HOUSING: At the edge of the city, where housing is clustered for light and view, skycars fly freely from one district to another.

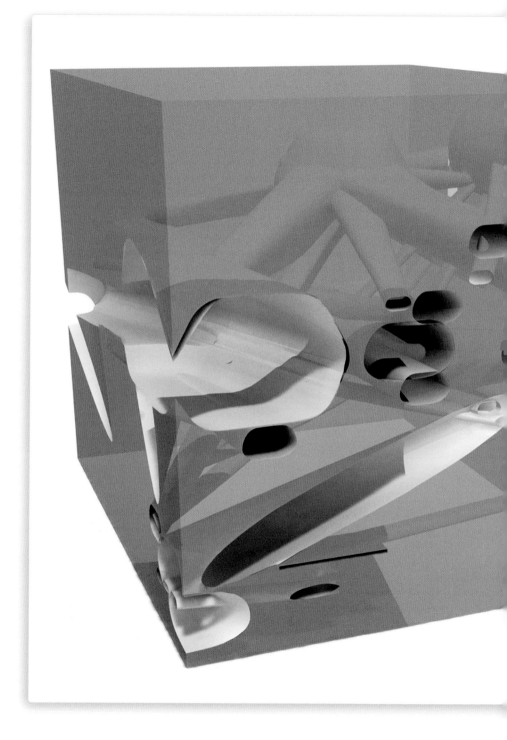

TYPE 2: **SWISS CHEESE CITY**

The Swiss Cheese city offers the densest arrangement of program and pedestrian potential. The city began as a solid block of program with skypaths boring through it. These pathways (skypaths) generate program deformations: The convergence locations of several intersecting paths produce large voids within the mass. Program is thus displaced by the open voids of the skypaths and intersections. This operation has the potential to support nearly 14 million residents within the same volumetric dimensions as that of Tower City, a scheme that accommodates only one third the population, or 5 million.

To ensure proper circulation among the hundreds of destinations, the pathway's network of tunnels necessitates an extensive and complex vascular support system of arteries, veins, and capillaries that serve primary tunnels. The Swiss cheese city is a continuous expanse of program that demands a secondary network of pedestrian pathways routing around the skycar paths.

The Swiss Cheese City has been excluded as a viable option for city development due to several problems. A severe lack of natural daylight and problems with air circulation are negative consequences of deep floor plates, measuring several hundred meters. Also, simple alterations in infrastructure would result in major complications, demolition, and ultimately, highly inflexible urban form. This city, as an extreme example of urban form enabled the studio to develop further studies.

People · 491,212
Skycars (2 per household) · · · · · · · 427,140
Built Program Volume (km³) · · · · · · 420.89
Size (m) · · · · · · · · · · · · · · · · · · · 800m3
Total Area (sq. m) · · · · · · · · · · · · 640,000
Total Volume (km³) · · · · · · · · · · · · 512.00
Program as % total volume · · · · · · 82.2%
%Total program · · · · · · · · · · · · · 287.24%
Neighborhood path volume (km³) · · 91.11
People per sq. km · · · · · · · · · · · · 767,518
Cubic m of program per skycar · · · · 985
Density Rating · · · · · · · · · · · · · · · 1st

Dispersed program (i.e school volume + coordinates)

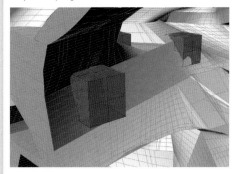

School volume absorbed

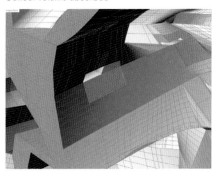

Mixed program potential

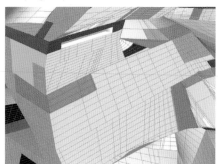

PROGRAM INCORPORATION The form of the Swiss Cheese city differs significantly from the original grid-based program distribution. Through an overlay process, the original grid distribution was absorbed into the mass of the new form. This example demonstrates a school, defined in orange, absorbed into a new mass. The school was then combined with parking strategies. At the intersection of a series of pathways, undulating void spaces are formed at light entry points (next page).

Absorbing program within a larger form offers a densely packed solid with limited possibility for natural light. The colored striations in this image indicate various program elements that have been absorbed into the mass and that assist in defining the flyzone.

The model photographs illustrate the relationship between program and pathway. Although the model is evocative in its layered, even airy quality, the built reality would offer a significantly different experience regarding natural light and ventilation. The model implies that the only source of natural light is from locations where the pathways pierce the exterior surface of the city.

People	182,686
Skycars (2 per household)	158,858
Built Program Volume (km³)	156.53
Size (m)	800m3
Total Area (sq. m)	640,000
Total Volume (km³)	512.00
Program as % total volume	82.2%
% Total program	106.83%
Neighborhood path volume (km³)	91.11
People per sq. km	285,447
Cubic m of program per skycar	985
Density Rating	2nd

TYPE 3: **CORAL CITY**

The Coral City achieved a density equal to that of the original distribution. This city utilized a set of rules at the micro scale to develop greater complexity at the macro, neighborhood scale. In developing the density, the program was offset from the paths, and then "echoed" at specific dimension dictated by the need for light and air, which produced zones of free-flight or less controlled movement.

The design of Coral City investigated several questions: How can a form be developed that responds to the skycar but does not possess the limitations of the previous two models of Tower City and Swiss Cheese City (i.e. an abundant open space with minimal response to the skycar and its movement in Tower City or a sacrifice of flexibility and many other beneficial requirements of a city in deference to the pathways in Swiss Cheese City.)

While previous methods of city creation responded to the need to displace program from paths or to carve pathways from program, neither method fully engaged the flight characteristics of the skycar. In Coral City, however, the relationship between program and pathway is more mediated. Much like Swiss Cheese City, the program surrounds the pathways, albeit in more limited fashion, and like Tower City, the controlled dimension of the program allows for needs of habitation. All buildings in the Coral City are directly accessible from all sides of the pathways, providing quick and convenient arrival at destinations. Furthermore, the depth of program plates creates a "back door" condition that provides access to a free-flight zone and greater access to other programs.

Methodology diagram

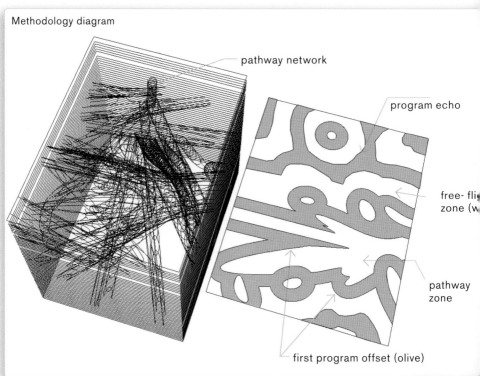

pathway network

program echo

free- fli
zone (w

pathway
zone

first program offset (olive)

The void spaces of Coral City are imagined as leisure zones or as hanging racks of parking. A network of pedestrian skywalks and parking "shelves" connect buildings together.

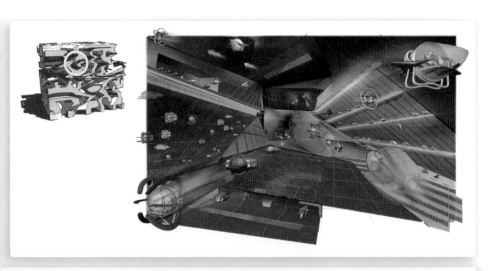

3 layers

10 layers

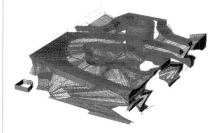

20 layers

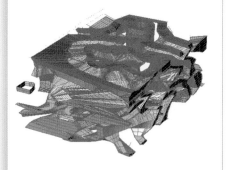

30 layers

40 layers

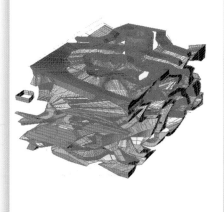

56 layers

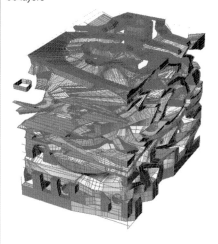

CORAL CITY /Formation Process (Connecting sections)

Program was placed in the interstitial zones between pathways. The city was then sub-divided into 56 plan sections and the program was offset from the pathway network at each level, producing a highly three-dimensional city of unanticipated complexity.
The program offset was then "echoed" to maximize densities, producing multiple layers, which could be carried to the city's edge. Such layers generated opportunities for back door conditions and free-flight zones in which the skycar might travel at slower speeds and within which unexpected relationships between program and pathway could occur.

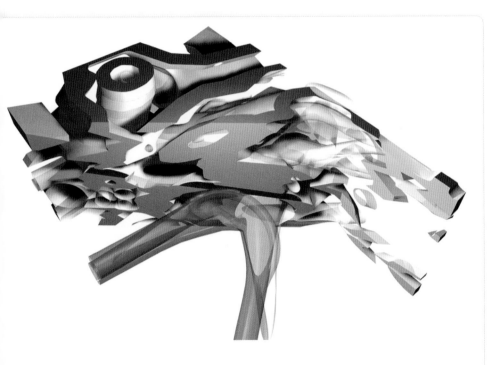

SECTION Section through city along tertiary path (red) connecting primary pathway network (blue) and free-flight zone (white).

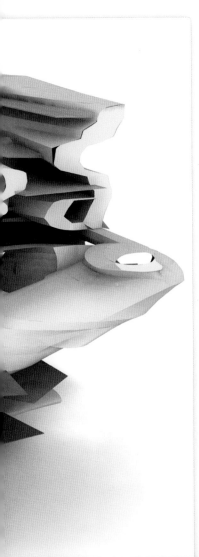

TYPE 4: **GARDEN CITY**

Though the Garden City utilizes a similar methodology as found in the Coral City, the Garden City eliminates the echo step so as to test a city type with decreased density and fewer uncontrolled flight zones. Accordingly, the formation of the Garden City relies heavily on the position and placement of pathways. This urban form contains skycar movement to the pathway network and surrounds the network with program. In isolating the movement, a pedestrian zone was created on the opposite side, producing a "garden" backyard. This garden zone encourages the use of individual forms of movements including: pedestrian traffic, skybikes, skymotorbikes, and skyVespas.

The size of Garden City began with a larger volume, now 1.5km x 1.5km (rather than 800m x 800m) that allowed the effects of paths outside of the previously defined volume of exploration. In the Coral City Model, leisure program was largely undefined, leaving many unanswered questions about its impact on organization and spatiality. The Garden City model accounts for these large leisure spaces, using them to weave no-fly zones together with leisure program to produce a corridor devoid of skycars and defined by terraces or "gardens" that fall outside of the program. As Garden City examined the role of the leisure/garden space, the previous role of the "free-fly" zone, as determined in the Coral City, was reconceived to heighten its purpose to pure pedestrian use as a no-fly zone.

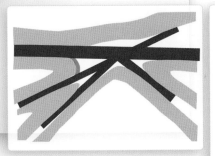

People	144,519
Skycars (2 per household)	125,668
Built Program Volume (km³)	123.83
Size (m)	800m3
Total Area (sq. m)	640,000
Total Volume (km³)	512.00
Program as % total volume	24.2%
% Total program	82.51%
Neighborhood path volume (km³)	91.11
People per sq. km	225,810
Cubic m of program per skycar	985
Density Rating	4th

GARDEN CITY /Formation process illustrated

Beginning with the initial pathways diagram, the overall volume of Garden City was increased. The program offset examined the potential for a greater range of pathway dimensions and subsequent void spaces. The pathway network varies by floor, producing a greater range of access and hence greater range of opportunity for diverse program form. The program form is made voluptuous and robust, through which green spaces are woven. The result of this formation process yields an armature for multiple no-fly zones / gardens to co-exist with program.

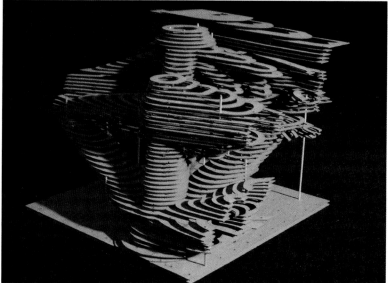

Pathway network

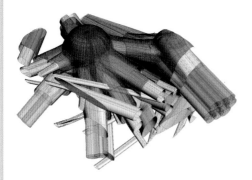

Program form

Program offsets

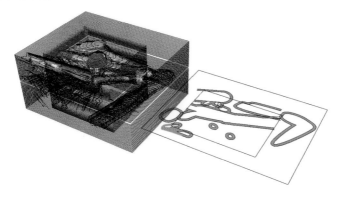

Gardens (leisure) placed

Program with garden space

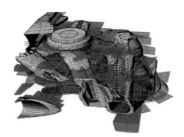

GARDEN CITY / Program Offsets

The Garden City offset method utilizes a more refined relationship between program and path to meet the requirement of the program for the neighborhood. Because the number of pathways and their size vary significantly throughout the 800m section of the city (from 1 small path to as many as 10-15 paths), a range of program may be served by each path. Therefore, if only one path served a horizontal section, more program can group around that path, producing a large offset. Similarly, near the city center, several large paths with smaller branches serve more program, so less program collects around the pathway and the offset is ultimately smaller.

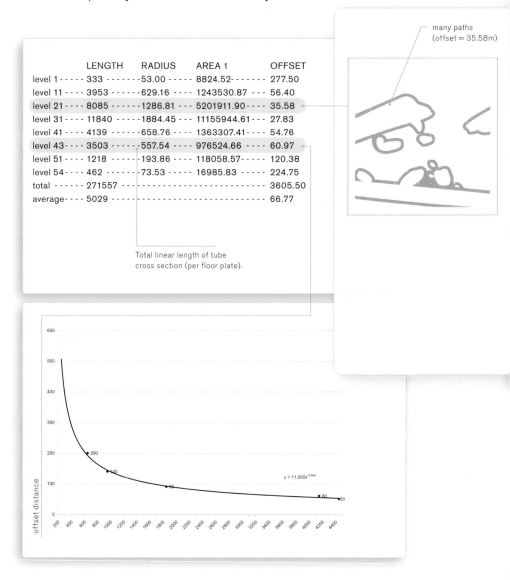

many paths
(offset = 35.58m)

	LENGTH	RADIUS	AREA 1	OFFSET
level 1	333	53.00	8824.52	277.50
level 11	3953	629.16	1243530.87	56.40
level 21	8085	1286.81	5201911.90	35.58
level 31	11840	1884.45	11155944.61	27.83
level 41	4139	658.76	1363307.41	54.76
level 43	3503	557.54	976524.66	60.97
level 51	1218	193.86	118058.57	120.38
level 54	462	73.53	16985.83	224.75
total	271557			3605.50
average	5029			66.77

Total linear length of tube
cross section (per floor plate).

$y = 11,000x^{-0.644}$

offset distance

Map of images

office node

university node

soccer stadium

office node

basketball arena

grassy zone

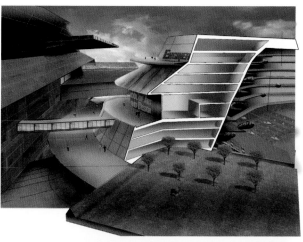

At the node of a university, the exterior or garden side is devoid of skycars and becomes a pedestrian campus. The interior of the node, at the confluence of several pathways, is lined with parking spaces.

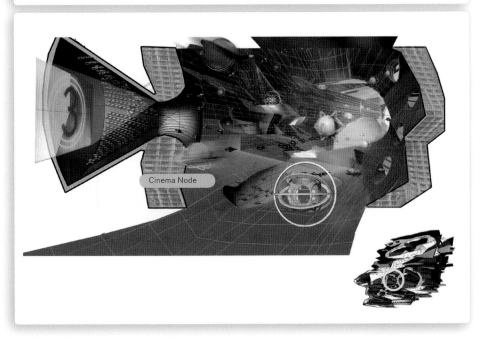

Cinema Node

FROM CAR(CITY) TO SKYCAR(CITY)

SKYCAR CITY EMERGENCE

Architects, urban designers, filmmakers, and artists have produced numerous urban visions that offer a rich backdrop against which to speculate on urban form. Charting the relationship between building form and height, energy consumption and production, population density and travel time, this timeline hypothesizes the trajectory toward skycar cities. As population and energy consumption (and subsequent congestion increase), alternative technologies emerge and buildings respond with escalating height. By 2100, oil supply and demand decreases and the prevalence of the skycar offers a direct impact on urban form.

OIL DEMAND /BARRELS ANNUALLY (BIL.)

OIL SUPPLY ANNUALLY (BIL.)

CO2 EMISSIONS /METRIC TONS ANNUALLY (MIL.)

COMMUTE TIME (MIN)

WORLD POPULATION (BIL.)

HEIGHT (M)

1500	1750	1760	1770	1780

[1490]
Leonardo da Vinci sketches flying machines and a helicopter.

[1755]
Discovery of carbon dioxide.

TIMELINE

Compares and speculates on a the potentials and origins of a sky based infrastructure.

PRECEDENTS

1790	1815	1840	1855	1870

TECHNOLOGY & TRANSPORT DEVICES

[3]
gofier Brothers
at the hot air bal-
, accomplishing
human flight.

[1801]
First steam pow-
ered vehicle.

[1830]
Establishment of steam
powered railroad network.

[1859]
Petroleum distillation
process initiates decline of
coal as a power source.

ENERGY, SCIENCE & HISTORY

[1790]
· Electric battery invented

· A patent is granted for the
battery, formalizing energy
as "portable."

[1830]
Electromagnetic
motor invented.

[1850]
Incorporation of the
Pennsylvania Rock Oil
Company, first American
oil company.

[1860]
US begins to export
petroleum to Europe.

FILM & FANTASY

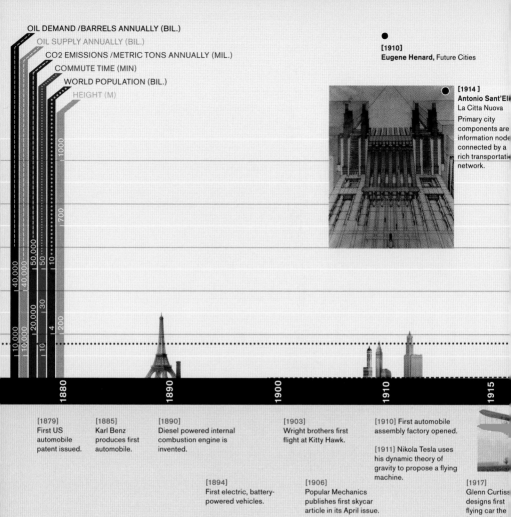

OIL DEMAND /BARRELS ANNUALLY (BIL.)

OIL SUPPLY ANNUALLY (BIL.)

CO2 EMISSIONS /METRIC TONS ANNUALLY (MIL.)

COMMUTE TIME (MIN)

WORLD POPULATION (BIL.)

HEIGHT (M)

[1910]
Eugene Henard, Future Cities

[1914]
Antonio Sant'Eli
La Citta Nuova
Primary city
components are
information node
connected by a
rich transportati
network.

1880   1890   1900   1910   1915

[1879]
First US
automobile
patent issued.

[1885]
Karl Benz
produces first
automobile.

[1890]
Diesel powered internal
combustion engine is
invented.

[1903]
Wright brothers first
flight at Kitty Hawk.

[1910] First automobile
assembly factory opened.

[1911] Nikola Tesla uses
his dynamic theory of
gravity to propose a flying
machine.

[1894]
First electric, battery-
powered vehicles.

[1906]
Popular Mechanics
publishes first skycar
article in its April issue.

[1917]
Glenn Curtiss
designs first
flying car the
"autoplane".

[1876]
Telephone invented.

[1895]
Electric streetcars
rendered obsolete.

[1905]
Photoelectricity
invented.

[1913]
Henry Ford
introduces the
concept of "mass
production".

[1897]
Electron discovered.

[1892]
Albert Robida,
Un quartier embrouillé

[1908]
William R Leigh,
Visionary City
A painter, Leigh
creates his
elevated, multi-
level city rich with
transportation
infrastructure.

[1913]
Harvey W Corbett,
New York Future

[1919]
Virgilio Marchi, Citta Superiore

[1927] Richard Neutra, Rush City Reformed

[1928] Walter Gropius, Wohnberg

[1929] Le Corbusier, Algiers
Corbu's plan for Algiers centered
on an elevated highway, where
infrastructure is developed in terms
of transportation and as
a shell for program.

[1930] Alexander Weygers,
Discopter City
Weygers shows San Francisco
overtaken by saucerlike
discopters. Every area of
surface is given over to parking.

[1931] Hugh Ferriss,
Metropolis of Tomorrow
Based on New York's
1916 zoning laws,
Ferris anticipated a
city with multilayered
transportation routes.

[1932] F.L. Wright, Broadacre City
Wright's vision of a fully suburbanized
"city" where all inhabitants own an
automobile. The architect also predicted
the widespread use of flying cars.

PRECEDENTS

1920   1925   1930   1935   1940

[1939]
First successful
rotary engine
helicopter flight.

**TECHNOLOGY &
TRANSPORT DEVICES**

[1921]
Tambier Roadable aircraft combines aircraft with wheels.

[1927]
AO Smith Automobile
opens first fully automated
assembly plant.

[1937]
Waldo Waterman
flies first car
nicknamed the
"aerobile".

[1941]
Residential
airpark
developed.

[1920]
Congress Creates the US Power
Commission to oversee energy
production.

[1920-40]
Construction of hydroelectric plants in the American Southwest.

**ENERGY, SCIENCE
& HISTORY**

[1926] Metropolis
Pioneer in cin-
ematic visions of
the city proposes
skyscrapers con-
nected by multi-
level transportation
network.

FILM & FANTASY

195

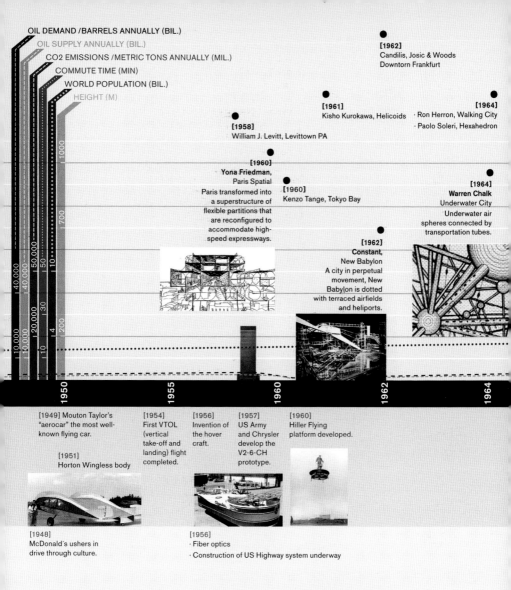

OIL DEMAND /BARRELS ANNUALLY (BIL.)

OIL SUPPLY ANNUALLY (BIL.)

CO2 EMISSIONS /METRIC TONS ANNUALLY (MIL.)

COMMUTE TIME (MIN)

WORLD POPULATION (BIL.)

HEIGHT (M)

[1962]
Candilis, Josic & Woods
Downtorn Frankfurt

[1961]
Kisho Kurokawa, Helicoids

[1964]
· Ron Herron, Walking City
· Paolo Soleri, Hexahedron

[1958]
William J. Levitt, Levittown PA

[1960]
Yona Friedman,
Paris Spatial
Paris transformed into
a superstructure of
flexible partitions that
are reconfigured to
accommodate high-
speed expressways.

[1960]
Kenzo Tange, Tokyo Bay

[1964]
Warren Chalk
Underwater City
Underwater air
spheres connected by
transportation tubes.

[1962]
Constant,
New Babylon
A city in perpetual
movement, New
Babylon is dotted
with terraced airfields
and heliports.

1000
700
50,000
40,000
50
10
40,000
20,000
30
10,000
10,000
10
4
200
1950   1955   1960   1962   1964

[1949] Mouton Taylor's
"aerocar" the most well-
known flying car.

[1951]
Horton Wingless body

[1954]
First VTOL
(vertical
take-off and
landing) flight
completed.

[1956]
Invention of
the hover
craft.

[1957]
US Army
and Chrysler
develop the
V2-6-CH
prototype.

[1960]
Hiller Flying
platform developed.

[1948]
McDonald's ushers in
drive through culture.

[1956]
· Fiber optics
· Construction of US Highway system underway

[1951]
UNIVAC-1 computer developed.

[1957]
First successful launch of man-
made satellite, Sputnik.

[1962]
The Jetsons
Driven skyward by ex-
treme pollution levels,
the Jetsons zoom from
place to place in family
sized flying saucers.

[1970]
Paolo Soleri, Arcosanti

[1966]
SPUR Asian City
of Tomorrow

[1969]
· Superstudio, Continuous
Monument Archizoom
· Archizoom Non-Stop City
· Mitchell & Boutwell
Comprehensive City

[1968]
Peter Cook, Instant City

[1967]
NER Group Urban Project

[1966]
Peter Cook, Plug-In City
Temporary programmatic
units are nestled within a
networked megastructure
fed by a vertical rail
system and cranes.

Among the earlier examples of skycar technology is the VTOL (vertical-take-off-and-landing) system employed by the Harrier Jet. This airplane is able to take off and land vertically, eliminating the need for a runway. It uses the Rolls Royce Pegasus Engine that is able to redirect thrust in the direction needed for the craft to hover and fly forward and even move backwards slowly in the air. Harrier jets have been used by the British Royal Air Force since 1969. The Moller M400 Skycar is a tilt-rotor VTOL craft currently in development for mass market. The first manifestation flew in 1989 and has gone through many iterations since. It is smaller than a Harrier jet, designed with civilian use in mind, and was recently posited by Popular Science magazine as being the possible car of the future.

[1989]
Tokyo Geotropolis

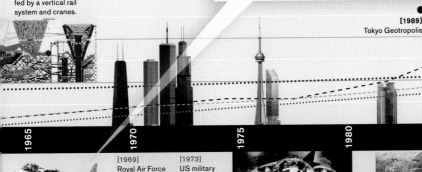

1965　1970　1975　1980　1990

[1969]
Royal Air Force
employs harrier
jet and VTOL
technology.

[1973]
US military
develops
GPS (Global
positioning
device).

Rolls Royce
Pegasus Engine

[1975]
Fourth Moller prototype: XM-4

[1989]
Fifth Moller prototype: M-200X

[1974]
Ozone layer vulnerability detected.

[1981]
First space
shuttle launch.

[1985]
Introduction
of consumer
mobile phone.

[1965]
Development
of the micro-
computer.

[1969]
First man walks on the moon.

[1970]
OPEC embargo initiates
"energy crisis".

[1982]
Introduction
of personal
computing.

[1989]
Launch of
the world
wide web.

[1978] Star Wars
A New Hope
Teeming with all types of air vehicles,
Lucas's Cloud City is the nearest
vision of a true skycar city.

[1982] Blade Runner
When flight capable
vehicles only available
to security forces,
citizens must travel in
ground based circula-
tion infrastructure.

[1989] Back to the Future
Fusion powered cars
travel through the city.

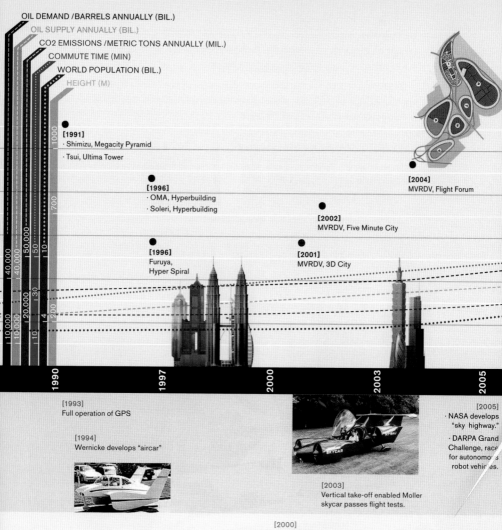

OIL DEMAND /BARRELS ANNUALLY (BIL.)

OIL SUPPLY ANNUALLY (BIL.)

CO2 EMISSIONS /METRIC TONS ANNUALLY (MIL.)

COMMUTE TIME (MIN)

WORLD POPULATION (BIL.)

HEIGHT (M)

[1991]
· Shimizu, Megacity Pyramid

· Tsui, Ultima Tower

[1996]
· OMA, Hyperbuilding
· Soleri, Hyperbuilding

[2004]
MVRDV, Flight Forum

[2002]
MVRDV, Five Minute City

[1996]
Furuya,
Hyper Spiral

[2001]
MVRDV, 3D City

1990 · 1997 · 2000 · 2003 · 2005

[1993]
Full operation of GPS

[1994]
Wernicke develops "aircar"

[2005]
· NASA develops
  "sky highway."

· DARPA Grand
  Challenge, race
  for autonomous
  robot vehicles.

[2003]
Vertical take-off enabled Moller
skycar passes flight tests.

[2000]
Dissolution of Global Climate Co-
alition. US administration denies
existence of problems.

[2001]
Soviet Soyuz space station
hosts first civilian "space tour-
ist" Dennis Tito.

[1997] The 5th Element
A fully 3D car chase
and dense city packed
with flying vehicles
and floating shops is
clearly influenced by
the visions of Leigh
and "Metropolis."

[2002]
Star Wars
Skycars and other floating
vehicles move rapidly through
a city of high towers.

[2002]
Minority Report
Cars run mostly on tracks
and parking is situated
directly in front façade
of dwellings.

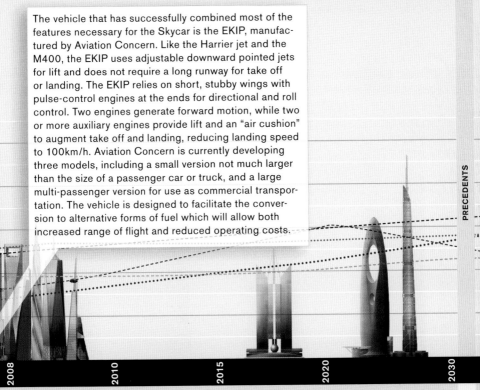

The vehicle that has successfully combined most of the features necessary for the Skycar is the EKIP, manufactured by Aviation Concern. Like the Harrier jet and the M400, the EKIP uses adjustable downward pointed jets for lift and does not require a long runway for take off or landing. The EKIP relies on short, stubby wings with pulse-control engines at the ends for directional and roll control. Two engines generate forward motion, while two or more auxiliary engines provide lift and an "air cushion" to augment take off and landing, reducing landing speed to 100km/h. Aviation Concern is currently developing three models, including a small version not much larger than the size of a passenger car or truck, and a large multi-passenger version for use as commercial transportation. The vehicle is designed to facilitate the conversion to alternative forms of fuel which will allow both increased range of flight and reduced operating costs.

2008   **2010**   **2015**   **2020**   **2030**

TECHNOLOGY & TRANSPORT DEVICES

[006]
elligent braking
stem appears in
oduction cars.

[2009]
Rocket Racing
League Debuts.
Pilots compete
on virtual tracks
with other
online gamers.

[2010]
Moller skycar enters
limited production.
Retail price
$750,000 USD.

[2020]
Jet turbine thrust
increased through
application of
nanotechnology.

[2030]
Self-piloting
cars become
widely
available.

ENERGY, SCIENCE & HISTORY

[2010]
· Fuel Cell stack capacity
reaches 3000 lifetime hours.

· Flying luxury hotel debuts.

[2015]
Cars possess
3-cyl engines and
20% are hybrids.

[2020]
· Global automobile
population tops one
billion.

· Atmospheric C02
levels peak at 38 tril-
lion metric tons.

[2030]
Fuel flexible
turbines are
invented.

FILM & FANTASY

2006] Robots
Robot City has a mass-transit system of flying pods.

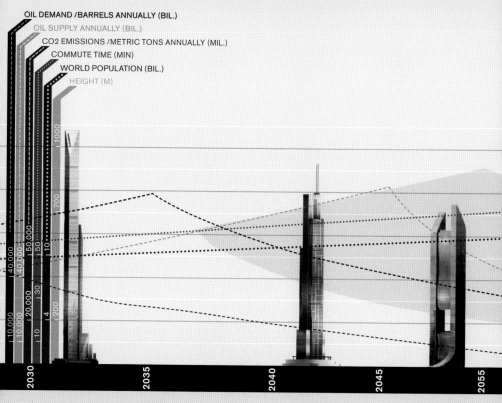

OIL DEMAND /BARRELS ANNUALLY (BIL.)

OIL SUPPLY ANNUALLY (BIL.)

CO2 EMISSIONS /METRIC TONS ANNUALLY (MIL.)

COMMUTE TIME (MIN)

WORLD POPULATION (BIL.)

HEIGHT (M)

2030 2035 2040 2045 2055

[2035]
Price of consumer
Moller skycar set at
60,000 USD.

[2035]
The reliance of biomass
energy on increasingly
scare fossil fuels initi-
ates its reduced use.

[2040]
In 25 years, use of
solar energy has
increased by 130%.

[2055]
Vast areas of the US
Southwest devoted to
solar farms.

[2050]
Commencement of
the construction of
a full-scale fusion
energy plant.

YEAR 2030 Skycars emerge as a viable alternative to ground-based
vehicles, eventually overtaking automobiles as the primary means
of transportation. Entire cities reorganize around the ever growing
use of skycars. Skypaths, initially crude flight zones, are refined and
ultimately develop into rule sets based on the new specificities of
skycars. Cities easily absorb the new vehicles as they pass freely
overhead. Densities decrease due to the new freedom of movement
and cities expand, creating super-suburban sprawls. As all vehicles
become flight based, the ground plane is no longer needed as the
primary means of movement and new uses for it are devised. The
ground fills up... and building vertically is an obvious response.

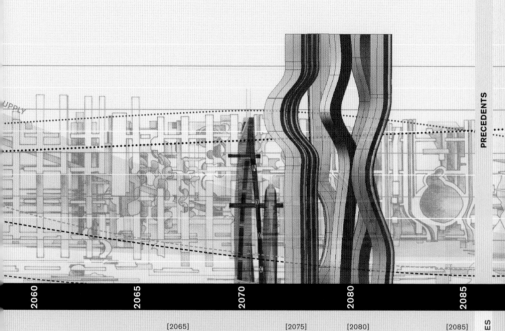

2060 **2065** **2070** **2080** **2085**

[2065]
Self-piloting personal air
vehicles ready for global use.

[2075]
Increased
skycar traffic
requires
development
of new safety
systems.

[2080]
Mass transit
becomes airborn.

[2085]
Skycar is the
dominant
form of urban
transporation.

[2065]
Electric fuel cell
predominates.

[2070]
Final petroleum
reserves
exhausted,
nuclear power
supplies 40%
of electricity
demands.

[2075]
Oil and gas
entirely
replaced by
wind, solar,
and tidal
energy based
systems.

[2080]
Atmospheric CO_2
content peaks.

[2060]
Population control
is primary concern
regarding earth
inhabitation.

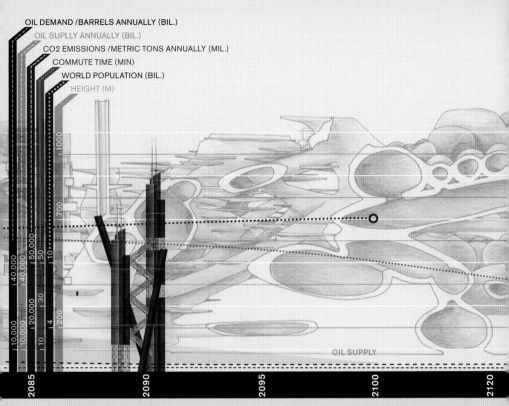

OIL DEMAND /BARRELS ANNUALLY (BIL.)
OIL SUPLLY ANNUALLY (BIL.)
CO2 EMISSIONS /METRIC TONS ANNUALLY (MIL.)
COMMUTE TIME (MIN)
WORLD POPULATION (BIL.)
HEIGHT (M)

OIL SUPPLY

2085   **2090**   **2095**   **2100**   **2120**

[2085]
Skycar is the
dominant
form of urban
transporation.

[2090]
Lighter, faster,
and more efficient
skycar achieves
360 mi/cell pack.

[2100]
City planning and
development center
around the skycar.

YEAR 2090 Cities project skyward as the previously
road-dominated ground plane is saturated with urban
program. Entrances and lobbies, advertisements and
action occur at 800 meters. The gridded patterns of
cities still persist from centuries-old ground based
movement and now clash with the new, efficient skypaths. Architecture responds by bending, leaning, and
twisting around skypaths for greater frontages. These
skyscrapers use one another for lateral support and
networks of paths and movement emerge hundreds
of meters off the ground. The grid is still apparent
and architecture mediates the clashing systems.
This 'Tower City' does not fully utilize the potential
of flying cars.

YEAR 2150 A datum of 800 meters caps the previous charge of upward construction. New solutions finally optimize the void space above and below the skypaths. Within several years the 'towers' of last century are lost in a tangle of program. The grid of the 19th and 20th centuries can only be found in pictures. The skypaths, once only electronic projects in a digital void, are now fully enclosed by clamoring homeowners, business entrepreneurs, and entertainment corridors. Everyone desires an address on the system. Parking, likewise, changes dramatically. New systems and types are necessary. Early editions of skycars land like airplanes; the newest skycars can link magnetically or slide onto prongs within the architecture. Secondary voids become free fly zones that serve hundreds of citizens with addresses in the sky. A city of canyons and a look of coral. These zones are undefined however and lack the full potential of program uses. The dark and isolated lower levels in the city are abandoned.

PRECEDENTS

2140   2160   2180   2200   2220

TECHNOLOGY & TRANSPORT DEVICES

YEAR 2210 The parts of the city that atrophy in darkness and isolation eventually fall to ruin; this includes most of the ancient 20th century structures holding onto addresses at ground level. Quality of life still dominates the city's organization: what was dark or decaying is discarded, and space not served directly by skycars is abandoned. Overtaking this city of canyons and coral is an efficient machine, clearly delineating the park from the road, the garden from the infrastructure. The two are inexorably linked in form and organization, however they never mix again. Everyone has their address both on the garden (free from vehicles), and also on the path (charged with skycar activity). Long gone are the earthbound transportation systems and the organization around the wheeled vehicle. These new cities can expand to cover the globe. Newer models of skycars and technology constantly offer the opportunity for more density and speed with the beauty of flight.

ENERGY, SCIENCE & HISTORY

FILM & FANTASY

CASE: TIANJIN, CHINA

While the hypothetical cities offer visions of possible future inhabitation, what are the effects of the skycar on an existing city? Can we imagine an urban development pattern? Using the city of Tianjin as a case study with rapid growth potential, the studio explored two urban models: suburbanization and urbanization. Both models were assumed to reach high levels of population and represented extreme versions of each case.

TIANJIN, CHINA [39.8N 117.10E]

These diagrams provide a means of understanding the existing circulation of the city. The studies serve as a foundation for an analysis of Tianjin and the relationship between urban form and modes of movement.

DENSITY

One of China's densest cities with one of its largest ports, Tianjin's trajectory for economic and physical growth is an ideal condition for the potential application of skycars. The city's rich history and existing urban fabric offer multiple hypotheses to explore the nature of skycars within an urban and suburban context. Given similar populations between Tianjin and Chicago, a satellite view reveals the comparative densities between the two cities.

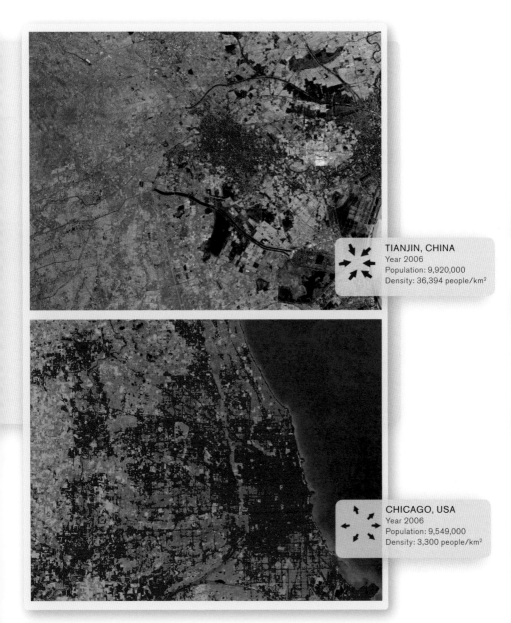

TIANJIN, CHINA
Year 2006
Population: 9,920,000
Density: 36,394 people/km^2

CHICAGO, USA
Year 2006
Population: 9,549,000
Density: 3,300 people/km^2

HYPOTHESIS 1: Super-Suburbanization

Skycars can traverse the entire central district of Tianjin in little over a minute. This new freedom initiates a significant suburban expansion of the city; it grows, spilling out into the countryside. Skypaths create direct connections between disperse destinations.

Suburbanization of Tianjin density, thousands of persons/km²

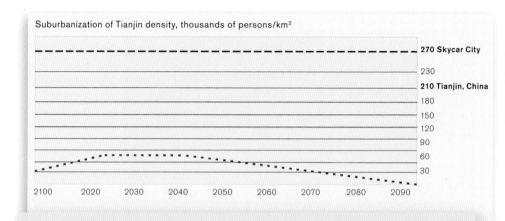

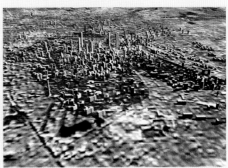

TODAY
Tianjin is a satellite site for the 2008 Summer Olympics, hosting events in a new stadium located on the city's outskirts.

2020
Urban growth patterns follow major highway ring roads of Tianjin.

2030
2030 Urbanism peaks. The skycar is introduced to Tianjin. Skycar acceptance is overwhelming. People can travel to destinations in a fraction of the time.

2040
Suburban developments intensify as the skycar allows people to live as far away as Beijing and Tanggu yet maintain an easy commute to Tianjin.

2045
The massive proliferation of suburbs establishes common routes of mass transit. The influx of skycars requires the development of skypaths and a skypath system that connects suburbs with straight, direct flight paths.

2060
Tianjin city center becomes an industrial/commercial city with visitors traveling from the suburbs into the city's center.

2080
As traffic increases, additional skypaths are added to the system. Paths are integrated with the city and influence further development.

2100
Super-suburbanization reaches its peak. The ability to travel between destinations is maximized.

In the Suburbanization model, the skycar would allow Tianjin's density to disperse throughout the country creating über-sprawl.

Yangcun
Qingguang
Tianjin
Junliangdeng
Jinghai
Xianshuigu
Yangliuqing
Tanguu
Xiaozhan

SUBURBAN NODES Within Tianjin province, there are nine suburban metro areas.
Each area supports a large population that is interdependent and dependent upon the city. Program in the Suburban model is widely dispersed and distributed into areas of singular program use. This model creates a wide tapestry of destinations.

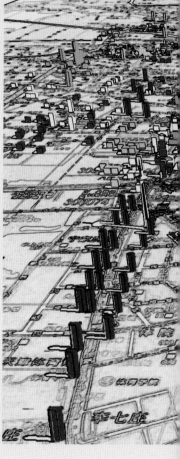

Leisure   Housing   Office

Healthcare   Education   Shopping

PATHWAY PROGRAM

Major destinations and nodes connected to each other create "sky highways" that would allow for swarming of multiple skycars in one path. The Suburban Pathways are defined by major destinations. The Pathways link destinations with the suburbs, and connect cities such as Beijing with other dispersed program. By connecting the destinations to the built structure of the suburbs, major zones of flight appear. With the ability to fly anywhere, anytime, major Skyways and Free-Flight paths emerge.

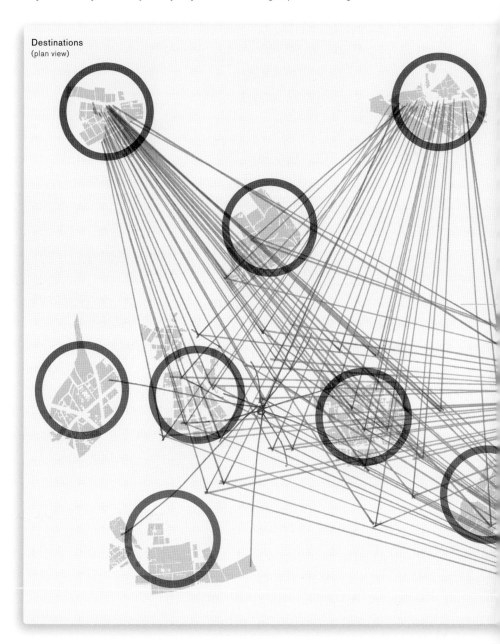

Destinations
(plan view)

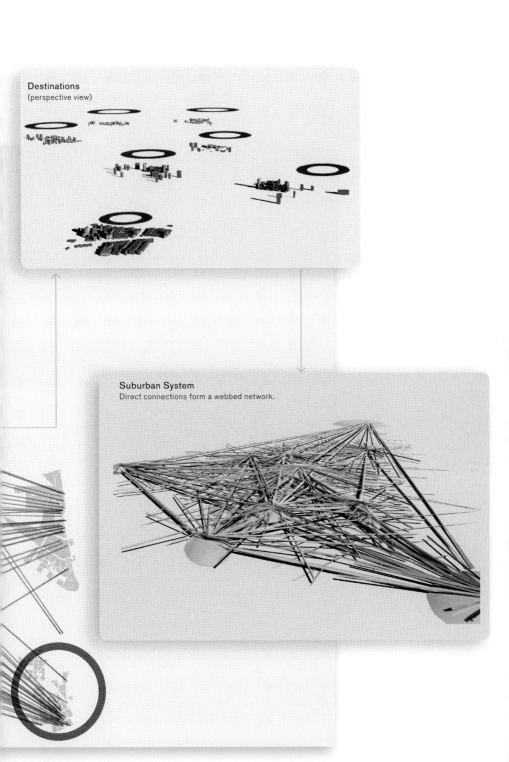

Destinations
(perspective view)

Suburban System
Direct connections form a webbed network.

SKY ZONING

Skycars increase travel speed and decrease commute time. Living outside of the city no longer requires lengthy commute time to work or daily destinations.

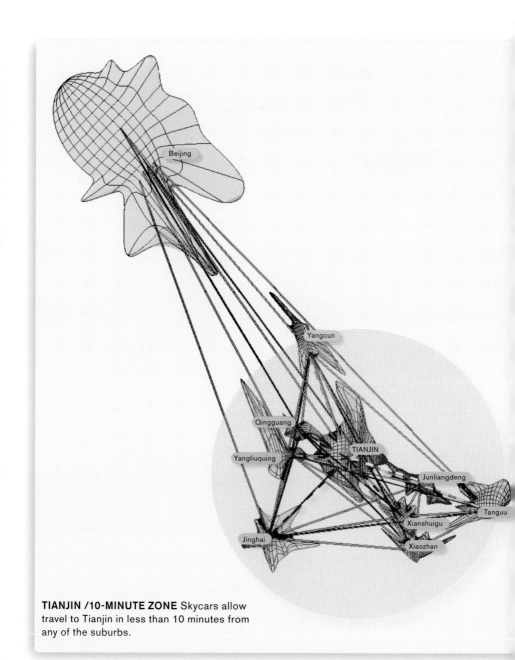

TIANJIN /10-MINUTE ZONE Skycars allow travel to Tianjin in less than 10 minutes from any of the suburbs.

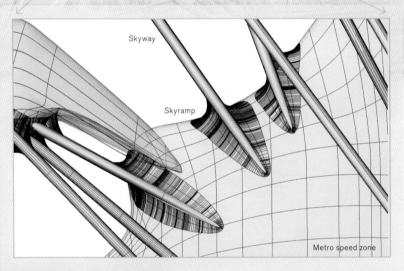

Skyway

Skyramp

Metro speed zone

SKYWAY 300 KM/HR MAXIMUM
The direct route from city center to city center. Expressways are the safest way for high-speed travel, providing carefully controlled highways with clear rules and regulations.

METRO SPEED ZONE 100 KM/HR
Zone is determined by density per square kilometer. Therefore, sky zones change to reflect urban change.

SKYRAMPING 800 METER RADIUS
Radius is based on safety buffer and turning radii of a typical skycar traveling from 300 km/hr to a reduced Metro speed zone of 100 km/hr.

A close-up view of a destination zone reveals the complex layering required to configure the skyway, the skyramp, and metro speed zones. In this view, several skyways that connect one destination to another hover above the metro speed zone.

Three types of zones organize skycar traffic: the skyway, the skyramp and the metro speed zone. These pathways and fields create an interconnected web of allowable flight areas with associated speed limits. The form of the web is driven by skycar speed, turning radii, and safety configurations.

HYPOTHESIS 2: ÜBER-URBANIZATION

The skycar allows the vertical expansion of Tianjin. As the skycar becomes the primary mode of transportation, it is necessary to carve skypaths through the dense urban fabric for efficient travel between destinations.

Destinations in Tianjin

2006
The density of Tianjin is ever increasing due to the city's importance as a primary port for China and its close proximity to Beijing.

2015
Buildings continue to grow vertically, especially around the expressways and the Haihe River.

2030
Skycar travel is introduced. Parking is poorly integrated, occupying roofs. Traditional transportation continues to occupy the highways.

2040
Skycars become popular due to excessive congestion of ground transportation.

Urbanization of Tianjin: Density, thousands of persons/km²

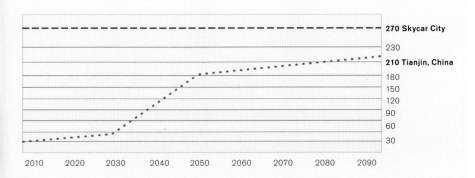

270 Skycar City
230
210 Tianjin, China
180
150
120
90
60
30

2010 2020 2030 2040 2050 2060 2070 2080 2090

2045
New urban codes require that skycar parking be integrated into building design.

2055
Tianjin becomes too dense for free travel. More direct and quick routes are required. Sky-paths are carved through the city.

2065
Highway land is sold as buildable areas. All automobile travel ceases to exist.

2100
Buildings lean on each other for structural support, allowing for the creation of extensive skywalk systems that form a pedestrian greenbelt around the city.

DESTINATIONS

Tianjin has many important nodes that define hubs of activity. For example, the Education node is comprised of two universities located adjacent to one another. The leisure node is the ancient, historic district of the city. Program in the urban model is densely packed and mixed, allowing for a closer concentration between destinations.

Urban Program Distribution

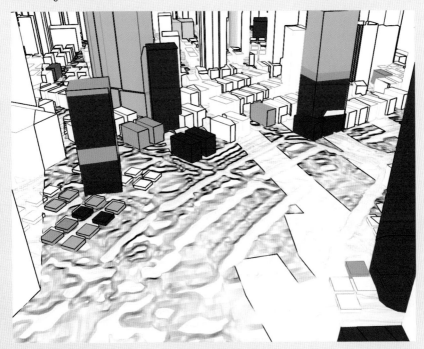

● Housing (38%)
Evenly dispersed
(average 8m2 per/person)

● Leisure (13%)
8 major parks
1 greenbelt
Olympic Stadium

● Office (8%)
30 largest companies

○ Healthcare (5%)
University hospital node
Hospitals

● Shopping (4%)
1 pedestrian mall
1 modern district

● Education (12%)
26 Universities
1000 high and
secondary schools
High-tech zone

● Industry (20%)
Port of Tianjin
Auto manufacturing
Petroleum
Marine chemicals
Textile and appliances
Agriculture
Airport

In the Urbanization model, Tianjin's density and vertical growth would alter dramatically.

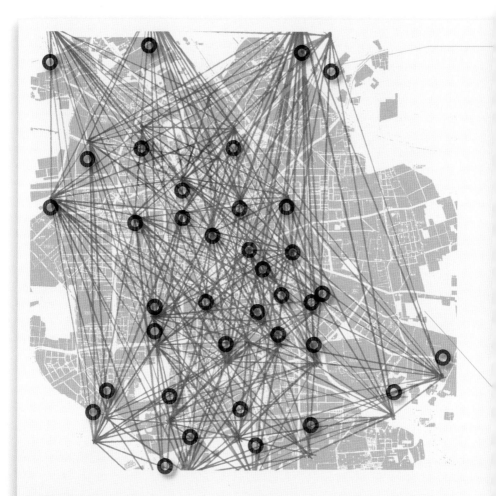

UNRESTRICTED TRAVEL As pathways connect all destinations, freedom of movement exists across the city, above and within the original urban structure. Existing buildings, topography, and streets affect the layout of pathways. Utilizing the original city structure yields connection to any number of possible destinations; areas of free-flight allow complete freedom of movement, while other areas remain restricted by existing buildings.

URBAN PATHWAYS

Destinations

City Structure

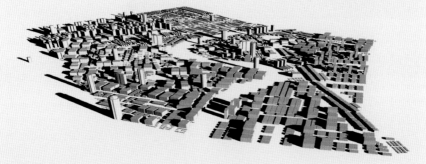

Pathways
*Tubes represent the invisible pathways of the skycar.

In the Urbanization model, Tianjin's density and vertical growth would alter dramatically. A major skypath above the Haihe River serves as a primary artery for the city. This dominant circulation tube is supported by a complex network of smaller paths that connect between primary and secondary destinations.

As the city's buildings grow taller, skypaths connect buildings at upper levels.

Depending on time of day and traffic volume, these tube paths vary in dimension.

10:00am

10:10am

10:05am

10:15am

PATHWAY CONFIGURATION Unrestricted Travel: Pathways are constantly changing, reshaping, and rearranging. The pathway volume is mutable dependent upon the quantity of skycars and its user.

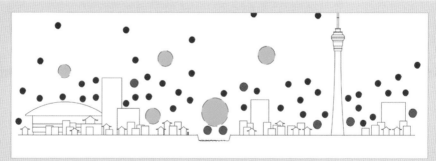
Speed Zones

PATHWAY PROGRAM DEVELOPMENT As Tianjin grows, future development must clearly delineate skypaths. Skypaths become a major factor in city planning and design such that building heights and accessibility are regulated; travel may remain unrestricted throughout the city. As the city matures, skypaths (indicated in green) are numerous, requiring greater bundling.

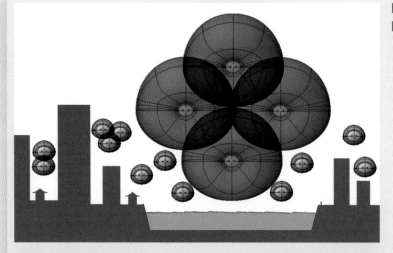

150 km/hr
50 km/hr

SPEED ZONES In areas of mass transit, such as skypaths above the Haihe River, it is possible for skycars to travel at higher speeds. The buffer zones require a minimum area for turning at prescribed speeds and thereby limit the spacing of cars in the cross section. Slower exit paths have smaller buffer zones.

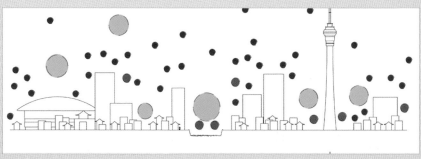

2055

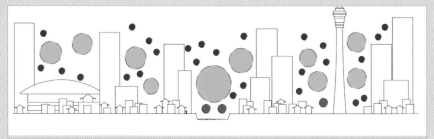

2100

PARKING Initially, skycar parking would adapt to the city structure. Parking on the roof or on the street would be obvious. However, as skycars begin to dominate urban life, parking will be integrated into buildings as a major design feature.

The application of the skycar to Tianjin hypothesized upon two methods of urban growth, a super-suburbanization and an über-urbanization. The density in the suburbanization model was dispersed over multiple outlying cities (annexing these smaller cities as neighborhoods within a large field) while the density in the urbanization model relied upon extreme vertical growth and a complex network of pathways to navigate the city.

With regard to the suburban model, the studies reveal that the pathway network emerges as a legible system, easily understood by the skycar driver based on distinct zones for speed and access. Many outstanding issues remain including the direct effect of this pathway web upon built form, as well as the economic impact of less efficient land use; however, the system appears to optimize the skycar's primary capability of high speed over long distance, making this model an attractive alternative for Tianjin growth.

With regard to the urban model, the studies reveal that the pathway network is chaotic and limited by the existing urban fabric. The pathway system likely requires a high degree of traffic regulation, suggesting that an intuitive cognition of the urban circulation may be difficult to grasp. While the system becomes increasingly more legible as the buildings grow taller and the skypaths hover above the "old" city, the effect of this growth on urban life at grade is not clear. Yet, the optimization of existing topographic elements, such as the Haihe River, for conversion into a primary skypath suggests a natural pattern for skycar infrastructure development. Additionally, the formal necessities of carved buildings which "lean" upon one another for structural support at upper levels is stimulating.

As with many studies which operate under extreme parameters and time constraints, the actual potential of skycar on a city such as Tianjin remains enigmatic. The studies propose ideas about the potential of skycar in an applied condition but do not as of yet suggest a conclusive resolution. As a skycar city, Tianjin development would likely hybridize both models in more nuanced form. Taken from the suburban model, for example, the conversion of smaller, surrounding cities to become the residential neighborhoods of Tianjin is easily imaginable. One could also conceptualize each smaller city as a distinct (and perhaps more singular) program type (i.e. Tanggu as a commercial district; Junliangcheng as a residential zone, etc.). This notion requires further, regional programmatic study beyond Tianjin. Taken from the urban model, the likelihood of extreme vertical building height is conceivable (precedents for which already exist). The potential of these tall buildings to become a loose constellation of civic nodes and/or transportation hubs with "lobbies" divorced from the ground plane, emerges as a stimulating consideration that produces an altogether new city cross-section. This idea coupled with a clearly defined skypath system creates new potential for land use, connections between cities, and overall urban organization.

ON BOIDS AND BEAUTY
GRACE LA

"Skycar City? The world of 2100?" With wry glances and smirks, the subject matter for the inaugural Marcus Prize studio generated a healthy dose of skepticism and indeed, may be the reader's response when pondering this book's intent. What kind of hubris allows designers to imagine this future world? Can we take this studio effort seriously? What studio design culture is required to fabricate this totally imagined territory? I take this opportunity to recount some pedagogical reflections upon the studio.[1]

1 The Marcus Prize Studio was led by Winy Maas and Grace La, the Dean's pairing of the prize winner and a UWM faculty member. Though we had not worked together previously, the teaching dyad optimized shared interests in transportation infrastructure and urban form.

The Marcus Studio efforts began as a speculation upon the notion of skycars in relation to the problems of density –a critical response to the ills of inefficient land management, inevitable fossil fuel depletion, and extreme population growth, among others. The studio spent several weeks gathering enormous amounts of data, confirming the likely production of the skycar; yet, this research remained fallow for the conception of the new, oneiric world itself. By temperament, the cynicism of the initial research provided a doomsday model of an imminent tabula rasa from which the skycar city would emerge as a fully-formed system. These early inquiries lacked any speculation of an urban design which might evolve systematically, organically, and more optimistically from the world as we know it. After a subsequent studio critique from Jeff Kipnis (with references to Robert Somol and Sarah Whiting's text on a "projective" vs. a "critical architecture[1]"), we embarked on our venture into the debate and into a design methodology of radical pragmatism, as associated with the Dutch and in particular, with MVRDV.[2]

The academic grounding of the studio shifted after the twelve students began to contemplate the possible characteristics of the skycar –the specific qualities of skycar movement, its turning radii, action, evasive maneuvering, its "features." The skycar design charrette encouraged the students to accept the implicit desire for an ultimate freedom of movement, divorced from the ground plane, navigationally and territorially independent. The skycar's behavior established the initial rules that defined and guided speculation upon the resultant physical form. The absence of site, either "cleared" or "constructed"[3] proved both challenging and liberating as the studio faced the Herculean task of constructing these parameters. Though the magnitude of this effort left little time to ponder socio-cultural factors or the politics of the new world, the research provided a limited set of variables for the Petri dish.

Some of these skycar variables included speculation on alternative energy sources, variations in speed, parking and vehicular seating arrangements, and concepts of swarming (i.e. related to the 1986 flocking allusions of Craig Reynolds's boids in his contraction of "birds + droids"). The combination of these

---

1 Robert Somol and Sarah Whiting, "Notes around the Doppler Effect and other Moods of Modernism," *Perspecta* 33: *The Yale Architectural Journal*, 2002˙

2 In his article *"Artificial Ecology,"* Stan Allen suggests that radical pragmatism "as distinct from a bland empiricism – distances [MVRDV] from the formulaic rehearsal of convention, but it also sets them apart from a neo-avant-gardism that defies convention for the sake of defying convention. A stubborn, unimpeachable logic yields improbable solutions." See Stan Allen, "Artificial Ecology," in *Reading MVRDV* (Rotterdam: NAi Publishers, 2003), 83.

3 In Carol Burns essay "On Site: Architectural Preoccupations," Burns argues for an amplified consideration of site beyond its convention as defined by a map or plan. In a quest to understand the site as "constructed," the studio was challenged to conceive of a site with infinite variability and imagined, non physical, speculation. See Carol J. Burns, "On Site: Architectural Preoccupations," in *Drawing, Building, Text*, ed. Andrea Kahn (New York: Princeton Architectural Press, 1996), 149-167

variables produced a speculative taxonomy of skycars that began to inform the very infrastructure of the city and to refine the necessary qualities of the skycar itself. The pathway research formed the most evocative diagrams in which the students' consideration of the details —the range of the required buffer zone and its impact on dimensions and methods of passing, merging, weaving— suggested a simple but powerful idea of an ever-mutable sky path. This example offered a tangible strategy for absorbing varying volumes of vehicles during peak and off-peak hours, and simultaneously, proposed an unpredictable, enigmatic city with no fixed points. Given a program of 5,000,000 inhabitants, the students experimented with the relationship between pathways and urban program, developing four hypothetical cities of remarkably different spatial experience (nicknamed: Garden City, Coral City, Swiss Cheese City, and Tower City).

The production of this work demanded a fundamental shift in studio culture, placing the designer emphatically at the intersection of highly collaborative environments, postulating on the current and evolving position of the architect to use his/her skills to transmute research into viable, consumptive, and above all, legible images of complex systems. In this case, as Stan Allen has suggested of the Dutch working method, "the architects project a loose fit between programme and form, leaving enough 'play' to accommodate the tactical improvisation of the users. The structure is left incomplete."[4] The images and diagrams presented in this book —some fractal, some whole, and certainly heterogeneous in collection— suggest an unapologetic framework for speculations on future global inhabitation, which might reveal their full potential over time, and where segments of the imagined world are believable, in an albeit primitive state.

The designer of skycar city considered the relevancy of various data (velocity, turning radii, buffer zone) in order to design a meaningful diagram (often describing a non-spatial condition). From this diagram, the designer then extracted a spatial construction for the city. To produce infallible results, our efforts on Skycar City's infrastructure admittedly would require an even greater interdisciplinary approach as well as time and funding beyond what one semester could afford. Yet, the achieved level of indeterminate experimentation revealed a profound cultural shift within the design studio that involved: 1) the necessary suppression of the individual design ego in favor of an interdisciplinary and collective immersion; 2) a reluctant acceptance that the production of research and diagrams would outweigh the work of traditional, object-oriented form-making; 3) the recognition of subjective influences subverting "neutral" data-gathering; 4) an unyielding responsibility to re-conceive the design process itself, so as to define and direct the operations of the collective.

---

4   Stan Allen, "Artificial Ecology," *Reading MVRDV*, (Rotterdam: NAi Publishers, 2003), 87.

For the student, the design of the skycar city was perhaps the most important outcome of the studio; delays toward achieving this objective caused by
the digression of "research" were exasperating. For the teacher, the desire
to stretch the studio's typical frame of reference (in this case, discovery of a
potential DNA for the urban condition) was the primary pedagogical intent.
Consequently, did the studio's gaze shift from the object-orientation of buildings
to the process-investigation of undercurrents? From individual design effort to
collective sensibility? From the analysis of known, physical conditions to the
scrutiny of ephemeral and invisible cues (i.e. speed, force, duration, frequency,
quantity, distance)? From the training of an aesthetic literati to the education
of a systems analyst? Is it helpful to consider Michael Speaks's proposition to
move toward a professional practice defined by "design intelligence, and not by
any formal, theoretical or professional identity"?[5]

In this line of questioning, Reynolds' commentary on "flocking" provides a convenient (and ironic) metaphor to describe the action of the Skycar City design
student. In his essay, Reynolds notes that the natural tendencies of flocks and
herds involve a desire to stay close to flockmates, to define a center mass, and
simultaneously to avoid collisions: and that "the basic urge to join a flock seems
to be the result of evolutionary pressure from several factors: …statistically im-
proving survival of the (shared) gene pool from attacks from predators, profiting
from a larger effective search pattern in the quest for food, and advantages for
social and mating activities."[6] In the skycar studio environment, where students
were electronically tethered together through a digital network, there was a
tangible shift in behavior from individual (sole author) to flock.

At times, the students' flocking action was so literally defined as to construct an
image en masse. Armed with multiple software programs and lined up behind
banks of computers, the students exchanged drawings back and forth, regularly
composing a singular image by sectioning the drawing into quadrants and then
skillfully rejoining the parts into one. This collective methodology required working within a defined set of parameters (i.e. stay close to flockmates) and thus em-
phasized the unimpeachable logic of previously-produced diagrams (stay close
to the center of the mass). As a result, the students gravitated toward collective
reasoning and negotiated responses to design decisions (avoiding collisions),
producing enormous amounts of work in a short period of time (profiting from
larger, effective search patterns). The students formed a veritable flock within the
physical confines of our studio and the digital boundaries of our network.

5   Michael Speaks, "Design Intelligence and the New Economy" *Architectural Record*, January 2002, 72-79.

6   Craig W. Reynolds, "Flocks, Herds, and Schools: A Distributed Behavioral Model, in Computer Graphics," 21(4) *SIG-GRAPH 1987 Conference Proceedings*, 25-34˙

A byproduct of the flocking analog of design methodology demanded that impartial research ideally serve as the basis for collective design and reasoning. While we hoped that the quest for the pragmatic would yield inherent neutrality, we learned that such a process was not easily established. The designer should carefully scrutinize and constantly question the creation of the "center mass" to which the flock adhered. If such an analysis were executed with the utmost care, the designer could successfully shift the public's judgment from aesthetic choice into the realm of a seemingly linear, naturally obvious, and highly reductive logic. This working method revealed that the diagram is central to the action of the architect. Though this concept is not unusual (very early in their architecture education, students are typically instructed how to use and generate a parti diagram or to distill a physical condition which defines a design problem), it was greatly intensified in our studio.

The Skycar City studio taught us that the very gathering of historical information (vehicular, urbanistic, technological) and quantitative data (program usage, numbers of people at localities, physical properties of movement) was not, in fact, impartial at all but rather dependent on the subjectivity, sensitivity, and skills of the individual researcher. Furthermore, the translation of this data revealed subjective decisions at every increment of investigation, where each author's graphic emphasis of one condition over another yielded numerous, and sometimes oppositional, interpretations. Thus, the students' formation of diagrams (serving as a basis for design decisions) outweighed the design of Skycar City's urban conditions. Formal intuition, absorbed into a collective identity, was not to be suppressed, but rather re-directed to create persuasive arguments —the skycar diagrams were imbued with the designer's irrepressible desire for interpretation and shaping.[7]

Taking notes on the pedagogy of boids exposed the notion that unimpeachable logic is a fallacy, that the neutrality of research and its subsequent graphics are skewed, and that architectural design cannot flow linearly or singularly, from that previously established logic, despite its intended rigor. The body which constitutes design intelligence must be further defined and expanded; it is enriched by such subjective qualities as inspiration, memory, intuition, experience, and ethics. While this position seems to counter Allen's description of the Dutch working method and to challenge Speaks's definition of design intelligence, I wonder if we could suggest that the combination of "radical pragmatism"[8]

7 In broad generality, UWM's students are known for their great productivity in the realm of form making and tectonic. For further commentary, see Grace La and Kyle Talbott, "Editorial Statement" *Calibrations: the Wisconsin Journal of Studio Architecture 2003*, 8-9.

8 Stan Allen suggests that the radical pragmatism is derived from "unimpeachable logic," "no fuzzy intuition, no 'artistic' expression, no metaphysical claims." See Allen, 83.

and naked bias (be it political, formal, social, aesthetic, etc.), may generate unpredictable, progressive results. Is there a productive tension between the algorithmic clarity of pragmatism (as represented by the boid) and the intuitive devices of beauty? Can design exist without subjectivity as its protagonist and its subsequent (and at times inadvertent) moral or political implication?

It was quite fruitful for the studio (amidst the gathering of invisible skycar data) to intervene in this research with highly individual, idiosyncratic play —i.e. with arbitrary experimentation that evolved from an un-tethered condition (anti-flocking). The individual deviation from the flock reminded me that the desire to separate is as robust as the desire to cohere, and this tension is the necessary agent to advance the exploration.[9] As exemplified by "program echoing," the design methodology of one student, this operation assisted in the production of the Coral City. Why "echo" program? "Echo" refers to the manner in which the properties of an imagined built form repeat multiple times to produce concentric rings of space (either void or filled), thus proposing a dimension to the built program that is sensitive to light, form, and movement. Coral City optimized the vehicular fly-zones as the generative geometry for built space, relying on light penetration to inform proportion (floor plate depth). Thus it would be misleading and overly simplistic to suggest that the images heretofore evolved purely or linearly from the diagrams; or, that they emerged from a simple amalgamation of diagrams without the designer's assiduous massage.[10] The operations and diagrams, incremental and subjective acts of design, created new sets of parameters to critique and adjust. The evaluation of Coral City, for example, resulted in another emergent form, Garden City.

The students of Skycar City have been transformed. They are acutely aware that the architect may reveal complex systems that influence design; they are keen to engage interdisciplinary research; they are open to the benefits of collaborative practice; they are anxious to participate in a global economy; they are quick to celebrate the pragmatic; they are roused by all things ludic; they are technically sophisticated in the digital world; they are fearless, uninhibited in their action; they find the design of highways and roads sexy. They believe, most emphatically, in the power of their diagrams. This conviction, however, is particularly powerful when mitigated by subjectivity, thereby sidestepping an overly deter-

---

9 The notion that flocking behavior consists of both coherent and deviant movement as two sides of the same coin is eloquently described in the "Brooklyn Pigeon Project" by Aranda / Lasch. See Benjamin Aranda and Chris Lasch. "Tooling" *Pamphlet Architecture 27* (New York: Princeton Architectural Press), 70-73.

10 The student editors played a significant role in formulating the formal language of the diagrams and renderings. Following this studio, some of these editors and other skycar studio students have engaged the study of generative scripting as an appropriate digital tool to investigate the potential new role of the designer as "spatial programmer." This tangent interest, as an offshoot the work of this semester, may form the basis for which data is collected, sifted, catalogued, ordered, and made relevant.

ministic response. In an effort to create a body of design intelligence which relies on data and research as the foremost generative source, our studio could not obscure the formal and instinctive gifts of the designer. Despite a desire for an outward perception of neutrality, we could not negate the metaphysical, subjective, intuitive, critical impulses.

I am reminded of George Baird's suggestion that "a number of important questions remain to be asked... before a truly robust and durable new professional stance will be able to be achieved."[11] In his essay on "'Criticality' and its Discontents," Baird closes his article wondering if the projective and the critical cannot be reconciled, and this line of pondering is most productive. While he points out that a supporting body of projective theory does not yet exist, perhaps this studio can serve as a case study on the inner workings (successes and failures) of the projective agenda. The studio also forecasts the necessity to re-examine, define, and direct the operations of the emergent collective and its potential —to design the flock's movements. After this semester, amidst discussion of the "pragmatic" or the "decorative," the projective vs. the critical, entropy or disentropy, and all the new forms of digital interface required to engage contemporary design practice, I am left to wonder about the fragile balance between boids and beauty.

Grace La

---

11   George Baird, "'Criticality' and its Discontents," *Harvard Design Magazine 21*, Fall/Winter 2004, 21.

CREDITS

CONCEPT
Winy Maas

STUDIO CURRICULUM
Grace La

EDITED BY
Winy Maas and Grace La

AUTHORS
MVRDV and The University of
Wisconsin-Milwaukee, School of
Architecture & Urban Planning,
Marcus Prize Studio

MVRDV
Winy Maas
(principal of MVRDV, Rotterdam)

UWM
Grace La (Associate Professor of
UWM, School of Architecture &
Urban Planning)

STUDENT EDITORS
Ryan O'Connor, Trevor Patt,
Nick Popoutsis and Andy Walsh

PARTICIPATING STUDENTS
Bryan Howard, Tony Janis, Nick
Moen, Ryan O'Connor, Ella
Peinovich, Trevor Patt, Nick
Popoutsis, Tarah Raaum, Gloribed
Rivera-Torres, Scott Schultz, Tuan
Tran, and Andy Walsh.
Additional thanks to Kevin Dunphy

FOREWORD TEXT
Dean Robert Greenstreet

INTRODUCTION TEXT
Winy Maas

BODY TEXT
Grace La and Trevor Patt

AFTERWORD TEXT
Grace La

TEXT EDITS
Grace La, Irene Hwang (Actar),
Winy Maas, Kevin Dunphy

STUDIO CRITICS
James Dallman (Principal, La Dallman
Architects); Bruce Dennert (Engineer, Harley
Davidson); James Dicker (Associate Professor,
UWM); Bob Greenstreet (Dean, UWM,
School of Architecture and Urban Planning,
Milwaukee, Wisconsin); Jeff Kipnis (Dean,
Faculty of Architecture, OSU, Columbus,
Ohio); Paul Krajniak (Executive Director,
Discovery World at Pier Wisconsin);
Linda Krause (Associate Professor, UWM);
Brian Peterson (Architect, Planning Design
Institute); Jacob van Rijs (Principal, MVRDV);
Pam Schermer (Associate Professor, Artist,
UWM); Rainer Schnable (Executive Vice
President, Brooks Stevens); Gil Snyder
(Associate Professor, UWM); Kyle Talbott
(Associate Professor, UWM);
Harry Van Oudenallen (Professor, UWM);
Nathalie de Vries (Principal, MVRDV,
Rotterdam); Jim Wasley (Associate Professor,
UWM); Brian Wishne (Chair, UWM);
and David Zach (Futurist, Milwaukee)

ADMINISTRATIVE SUPPORT
UWM School of Architecture & Urban Planning
Administration and Staff; Lisa DiSalvo, Joe
Fieber, Steve Heidt, Kurt Meingast, Dee
Nordgren, Davey Singer and Janet Tibbets

STUDIO DOCUMENTATION, PHOTOGRAPHY, FILM
Mike Marianek and Adam Goss,
Spirit of Space

THE MARCUS PRIZE IS SPONSORED BY
the Marcus Corporation Foundation

BOOK DESIGN
Marieke Bielas, David Lorente, Actar

EDITORIAL COLLABORATION
Irene Hwang, Actar

DIGITAL AND PUBLISHING PRODUCTION
Oriol Rigat, Joan Fusté, Actar

FIRST PUBLISHED IN 2007 BY

Actar Barcelona, New York
www.actar.com
info@actar.com

PRINTING
Ingoprint S.A.

ISBN
88-208041-6-6

DL
B-39555-2007

Printed and bound in
the European Union

CONTACT

MVRDV

MVRDV
Winy Maas
Dunantstraat 10
3024 BC Rotterdam
PO Box 63136
Rotterdam / The Netherlands
Tel +31 10 4772860
Fax +31 10 4773627
info@mvrdv.nl
www.mvrdv.nl

UNIVERSITY of WISCONSIN | CELEBRATING
UWMILWAUKEE | 50 YEARS

UWM SCHOOL OF ARCHITECTURE
& URBAN PLANNING
Grace La
University of Wisconsin - Milwaukee
School of Architecture & Urban Planning
2131 E. Hartford Avenue
Milwaukee, WI 53201-0413
USA
Tel +1 414 229 4014
Fax +1 414 229 6976
gla@uwm.edu
www.uwm.edu/sarup

THE MARCUS PRIZE

MARCUS PRIZE
University of Wisconsin - Milwaukee
Office of the Dean
School of Architecture & Urban Planning
2131 E. Hartford Avenue
Milwaukee, WI 53201-0413
USA
Tel +1 414 229 4016
Fax +1 414 229 6876

DISTRIBUTION

Actar D

Actar D
Roca i Batlle, 2-4
E-08023 Barcelona
Tel +34 93 417 49 93
Fax +34 93 418 67 07
office@actar-d.com
www.actar-d.com

Actar D USA
158 Lafyette Street, 5th Fl.
New York, NY 10013
USA
Tel +1 212 966 2207
Fax +1 212 966 2214
officeusa@actar-d.com